Para May Harris,
amiga linda
con amor y respeto,
Imelda Delgado
April 20, 2013

An Intimate Portrait of Sidney Foster

Pianist . . . Mentor

Imelda Delgado

HAMILTON BOOKS

A member of
ROWMAN & LITTLEFIELD PUBLISHERS, INC.
Lanham • Boulder • New York • Toronto • Plymouth, UK

Copyright © 2013 by
Hamilton Books
4501 Forbes Boulevard
Suite 200
Lanham, Maryland 20706
Hamilton Books Acquisitions Department (301) 459-3366

10 Thornbury Road
Plymouth PL6 7PP
United Kingdom

All rights reserved
Printed in the United States of America
British Library Cataloging in Publication Information Available

Library of Congress Control Number: 2012951374
ISBN: 978-0-7618-5934-5 (clothbound : alk. paper)
eISBN: 978-0-7618-5935-2

∞^{TM} The paper used in this publication meets the minimum requirements of American National Standard for Information Sciences—Permanence of Paper for Printed Library Materials, ANSI Z39.48-1992

To the Memory of
Narciso and Polly Delgado
and
Blaise Montandon,
Beloved Parents and Teacher

Contents

Foreword   ix
   Charles H. Webb

Preface   xi
   Imelda Delgado

Acknowledgments   xiii

PART I. BEGINNINGS

Early Years	3
Composer	8
The Leventritt	12
After the Leventritt: The LeRoy-Foster-Scholz Trio	16
Sidney Foster and Norman Dello Joio	19
Stages Where Sidney Foster Walked	23
Evolution of Programming	27
Orchestral Soloist	34

PART II. FOSTER'S PIANISM

Russian Roots, Russian Legacy	41
His Hands	43
His Piano Teachers	46

Where He Taught	47
The Pedagogue	51
Collaborator—Indiana University	57
The Concert Pianist and the Old World Scholar (*An Unusual Partnership*)	60
Architect of Piano Performance Doctorate	61

PART III. PERSONALS

John	67

Five Women in His Life

Anna Diamond Foster and Dorothy Foster DiFazio	68
Mana-Zucca (1891-1981)	70
Isabelle Vengerova (1877-1956)	72
Bronja (Miss Bronja Singer/Mrs. Sidney Foster)	74
From the *Grande* Scale to Gourmet Suppers	76
A Little Potpourri	81

PART IV. DEFINING PERFORMANCES

Memorial to His Father, Louis (1937)	87
Concerto Highlights (1954)	88
From Fliere to Foster: To Russia, with Love (The Russian Tour, 1964)	90
The Boston Premiére of Bartók's Third Piano Concerto (April, 1965)	96

PART V. FINALE

1976: A Bicentennial and a Centennial	101
The Final Curtain	103
A Farewell Letter	108
February 7, 1977	109

Appendix A. In His Own Words: A Piano Workshop — 113

Appendix B. The Students Speak — 120

Appendix C: *Cadenza* to the Beethoven *Piano Concerto No. 3 in C Minor, OP. 37,* 1941 — 170

Index — 177

About the Author — 183

Foreword

The death of Sidney Foster on February 7, 1977, at the age of 59, left a gaping hole in the world of music and certainly in the faculty of the Jacobs School of Music of Indiana University. His performance, his scholarship, his teaching, and his artistic personality made indelible impressions on all who had had the privilege of coming in contact with this consummate artist.

A biography of Sidney Foster is long overdue. Imelda Delgado has made a valuable contribution to the literature of musicians by gathering in one volume details of an interesting, contributing, world-class pianist, whose life was dedicated to the highest standards of musical knowledge.

The great Josef Hofmann heard Sidney when he was ten-years-old, immediately recognized genius and suggested that he study at the Curtis Institute of Music in Philadelphia, where he became the youngest student ever admitted at that time. As the first winner of the Leventritt Competition in 1940, he was awarded a debut with the New York Philharmonic. The then eight New York newspapers praised this extraordinary achievement with glowing reviews. The *New York Times* under its headline, Ovation to Foster, noted his "brilliant playing with all the enthusiasm and fire of youth" and called him "a richly gifted performer whose approach to the keyboard was of the noble, heroic type."

Some years later, *Musical America* reviewed one of his Carnegie Hall concerts and proclaimed: "Sidney Foster is a virtuoso in the true meaning of that word. The piano sang again as it used to when the great masters of the past were at the keyboard." The *New York Times* said: "one of America's best pianists, whose art is in the great tradition of Rachmaninoff, Hofmann and Lhevinne."

Tours in the major music capitals of the world met with outstanding success, but Sidney also was deeply committed to giving young people some of the enormous gifts that he himself possessed. A brief teaching stint at Florida State University led to an appointment in 1952 to the faculty of Indiana University Jacobs School of Music. It was there that he made his brilliant reputation as a teacher of extraordinary capacity.

I had the good fortune of being his student in a class of Romantic piano literature during my first semester as a student in the doctoral program of piano at Indiana University, as well as his private student several semesters later. Immediately, his breadth of knowledge, his amazing ability to inspire, and his sensitivity to the individual needs of every student became apparent to each person in the class. Recognition of his brilliant teaching skills came with The Frederick Bachman Lieber Award, Indiana's highest teaching award, bestowed on Sidney Foster in 1975. The following year he was named Distinguished Professor, the ultimate professional rank given by Indiana University.

In this book you will hear first hand from students all over the world who have benefited from the dedicated, remarkable teaching of Sidney Foster. We were all touched by his sincerity, his deep sense of fairness, his encouragement of diverse points of view, his brilliance in teaching technique and musicianship at the same time, his gentle humor, and his never-ending devotion to thousands of students.

Sidney Foster's life was cut short by a devastating illness. But his contributions to the world of music will never be forgotten, and this volume will breathe new life into an amazing musical adventure. As one colleague aptly put it, "Sidney Foster could develop a student from 'an awkward, tense and clumsy player into a facile, fluent and relaxed one.' Every student he took under his wing, whether very talented or not so talented, progressed and improved by leaps and bounds."

There is really nothing more to be said. Read here with great pleasure how it was done!

Charles H. Webb, Dean Emeritus
Indiana University Jacobs School of Music

Preface

The establishment in 1924 of the Curtis Institute of Music in Philadelphia began a notable re-energizing in music performance in the United States. Philadelphia's Curtis Institute of Music became a magnet for the magical performers from the world's concert stages: Josef Hofmann, Marcel Tabuteau, Leopold Stokowski and many others whose artistic ideas were passed on to the students who were accepted at the conservatory.

By the late 1930's, some of those Curtis students migrated to Manhattan where they became world class contributors through their talents. Sidney Foster, Abbey Simon, and Jorge Bolet were a representative young trio of pianists from Curtis who continued their friendship in New York despite the fact that sometimes they would compete for the same 'prize.' Those three young pianists, and several others who began careers as Steinway artists, would transfer their artistic affiliation to Baldwin, a company that would go to extraordinary lengths to secure fine instruments wherever concert venues materialized. Interestingly, all three would ultimately teach at Indiana University where they inspired the next generation of pianists.

Sidney Foster was a spectacular, consummate artist; a concert pianist who possessed all the requirements for music-making: technique, temperament, intellect, originality. But at one time, that former Indiana University Distinguished Professor of Music confided to one of his graduate students that "I wanted to be a composer but became sidetracked after I won the first Leventritt Piano Competition in September 1940 when I was twenty-three."

Unlike some performers, Mr. Foster continued developing artistically as he matured. His name, although not a familiar one, was acknowledged and revered by connoisseurs. He was just fifty-nine when he died. According to those closest to him—his wife, his children, some observant friends and students—*today* was what mattered most to him. Yesterday's events were in the past. He did not dwell on them, be it a concert review or whatever else many of us continue to contemplate. This is not to say that he did not learn from the past. He did.

Early in his career Foster enjoyed a full-fledged and lively concert schedule. The young and handsome pianist was a highly sought concert artist. Though his life was relatively short, and as he developed a following as a master teacher, he never lost his passion or nerve to play music to live audiences. Significantly his last public appearance was with a new addition to his repertoire, a piano concerto that he had rediscovered: the Ernest Schelling *Suite Fantastique for Piano and Orchestra, Op. 7*, a formidable four-movement work deserving of the concerto label. He performed it three times in the fall of 1976, most notably with the Dearborn, Michigan Symphony Orchestra, the Indianapolis Symphony Orchestra, and the Bloomington Orchestra.

Differing from other artists of greater name recognition and fame who stop concertizing years before they pass on, Sidney Foster continued to learn and expand his solo repertoire to the very end. Having performed the Schelling in October, just three months before he died, he began studying the *First Piano Sonata in D minor* by Sergei Rachmaninoff, a rather difficult work. Foster's last performance to a live audience was of that piece in early December 1976. It was played to an audience of one in a university piano studio. As that individual described it,

> "The last time I saw Sidney Foster was at a lesson which began in a darkened studio. After a few pleasantries were uttered, he asked if I would like to hear the Rachmaninoff Sonata he had been learning."

Foster's choosing to learn that Russian work was significant as it underscored his love for that composer's works, and coincidentally or subconsciously, it was a harkening back to Foster's Russian roots.

The loss of one's precious mentor is devastating. But nevertheless and most significantly, a mentor's legacy continues through those individuals who studied with him. Even if he had lived long enough to write an autobiography, I believe that he would not have written one. Writing about Foster's yesterdays is an assignment I have given myself because yesterday's lessons with him, musical ones and otherwise, shaped my life and that of many others mightily and positively.

Imelda Delgado
Corpus Christi, Texas
April 10, 2010

Acknowledgments

Since my first awareness of Sidney Foster, I subconsciously began to index information about him. Through the years the collection in my mind and in actual documents—short notes, letters, concert programs, and so forth—accumulated impressively. As time passed—three decades since his death—an undeniable idea surfaced: I had to organize my thoughts about this teacher/mentor in writing. But none of us function without outside assistance; as I began to write I called upon many who assisted willingly and most generously. I gratefully thank the following:

Mr. Gino Francesconi, Carnegie Hall Archivist
Ms. Kathleen Sabogal, Manager, Carnegie Hall Archives
Mr. Richard Wandel, Associate Archivist, New York Philharmonic
Ms. Sally Branca and Susannah Thurlow, Curtis Institute of Music Archivists
Dr. David Lasocki, Head of Reference Services, Indiana University Music Library
Ms. Marilyn Graf, Archivist of Traditional Music, Indiana University
Dr. Henry Upper, Administration Executive, Associate Dean Emeritus, Indiana University
Dr. Charles H. Webb, Dean Emeritus, Jacobs School of Music, Indiana University
Dr. Mary Wennerstrom, Associate Dean for Instruction, Indiana University
Mr. Henry Steinway, Steinway Pianos, New York City
Ms. Vicki Silvera, Head of Special Collections, Florida International University, Miami
Mr. and Mrs. David and Irene Abosch, Musicians, Littleton, Colorado
Dr. J.B. Floyd, Professor of Piano, University of Miami, Florida
Mr. Abraham González, Researcher and Musician, Corpus Christi, Texas

Mr. Abbey Simon, Concert Pianist
Mr. and Mrs. Norman Dello Joio, Composer
Parkdale Printing of Corpus Christi, Texas, and Ms. Jenney Gunnar Arévalo
Jo Beth Holbrook, Secretary, Driscoll Children's Hospital, Corpus Christi, Texas
Dr. Evelyn McCarty, Friend, provided assistance with manuscript
Dr. Gustavo Valadez Ortiz, Friend of the family, provided editing assistance on the manuscript
Larry M. Dahl, Friend of the family, provided assistance formatting the computer manuscript
Dr. Edgar L. Cortés, Imelda Delgado's Supportive Spouse
Mr. Ray Paz, Pianist, Transcriber of Cadenza
Mr. John Gibson, Linear Music
Winifred Berner Parker, M.D.
Dora Koutelas, opera singer who provided useful suggestions for the manuscript
Mr. Donald Manildi, curator of the International Piano Archives at the University of Maryland

AND ESPECIALLY TO THE FAMILY OF SIDNEY FOSTER:

Mrs. Bronja Foster (wife of Sidney), Justin Foster (son), and Lincoln Foster (son)
Mrs. Dorothy (Dottie) Foster DiFazio, sister of Sidney Foster, who provided family photos, letters, and her recollections of the Foster family

Part One

BEGINNINGS

Early Years

Composer

The Leventritt

After the Leventritt: Leroy-Foster-Scholz Trio

Sidney Foster and Norman Dello Joio

Stages Where Sidney Foster Walked

Evolution of Programming

Orchestral Soloist

Early Years

At age three, all that Sidney Earl understood was how much he enjoyed playing his father's upright piano. He could barely reach the keys while standing. However, John, his babysitter, stacked many big books into a makeshift piano bench so he could reach and run his small hands all over the black and white keys just like his father. The first music Sidney heard was his father's playing and, within his ears' range and easy for him to pick out, the music broadcast from a radio.

Although his mother Anna did not play any instruments, she sang simple songs, and most importantly, she realized that her husband needed an outlet to relax by from his arduous family business. So she gifted Louis with an upright piano.

Sidney's parents, Anna and Louis, came from very different backgrounds. Louis Finkelstein was one of many brothers and sisters whose parents immigrated to the United States from Kiev via Ellis Island in the late 1800's, shortly after Russian radical revolutionaries assassinated Tsar Alexander II in 1881. Anna Diamond was an only child, born in the United States, shortly after her parents left Poland. From Ellis Island, Louis and his family went to Jacksonville, Florida, where other relatives had established themselves earlier. But after Louis became old enough, he detached himself from his family. He found his way to South Carolina, where he formed his own business in 1914 as a jeweler and pawnbroker. At that time, he married his sweetheart, Anna Diamond. His business in Florence, South Carolina, was known as the 'Florence Loan Office,' on East Evans Street.

Both Anna and Louis worked long hours in their business. In 1917, three years after they married, Sidney was born. Two years later, Edwin arrived. In 1921, a third son, Harold (known as Billy), was born, and Dorothy (Dottie) made her appearance in 1923. Even with this family of four children, Anna continued to work side by side with Louis. Once widowed, grandmother Diamond lived with the family, cooking for them, and managing their household. In addition, Anna found a young, caring Negro named John who babysat the growing family and serendipitously became little Sidney's music coach and collaborator.

While the parents worked, Sidney and sitter John developed their own music enterprise: Sidney glided over the old upright keyboard while John created percussive rhythms on overturned pots and pans. One late afternoon the debut of this dazzling duo was served up to mother Anna in her living room. "Ready?" whispered John to Sidney, as Anna opened the front door. The two began a most *bounciferous* rendition of *Yes, We Have No Bananas!* Anna had no music training or ambition. She had never heard her three-year-old play the piano, but from that day on she became her son's most loyal fan.

With sitter John's encouragement and his mother's stacks of books, Sidney continued playing by ear music he heard on the radio and music he imagined. The composer was born! The improvisations he delighted in working out were caricatures of people he saw—a practice much like that of the great Frédéric Chopin. He also developed stylistic pieces, some that sounded Spanish in rhythms, and some with melodic modes like those of the Native American Indians, undoubtedly resembling what he had heard on the radio.

Sidney had perfect pitch. He could play anything back that he had heard on his family's gramophone. Even if he hadn't had lessons, he nevertheless developed a following in Florence, South Carolina, his home town. Significantly, around the time he was five years old, a ladies' club engaged him to play for them: his first concert date. They paid him the grand fee of five boxes of sparklers!

In 1925, the family of six moved to Miami, Florida, where father Louis expanded his business to include ventures in real estate. Anna busied herself by researching various schools and a music education for all four of her children—piano lessons for Sidney, Edwin, and Harold, and ballet classes for Dorothy. Edwin was also given cello lessons, which he continued in New Orleans and later in Minneapolis.

Louis and Anna did not share the same attitude about music as a profession. According to Dorothy DiFazio, Sidney's sister,

> Father enjoyed music, but he believed that 'Music was for fun.' A career in music was outrageous. Any and all music was put away when father Louis came home from his often eighteen-hour work days. The driving force and clearing house for us to pursue our music seriously came from Mother. She looked for study and performing opportunities relentlessly and for advocacy from patrons of the arts wherever we lived.

Early Years

Sidney attended the Shenandoah Elementary Public School and took piano lessons from Earl Chester Smith at the University of Miami's Conservatory. During that time in Miami, Josef Hofmann, considered one of the greatest pianists at the time and Director of the Curtis Institute of Music, heard Sidney play. His strong endorsement assured Sidney's acceptance to the Curtis Institute of Music as a ten-year-old child. Thus, he became one of a handful of young children that enrolled at the Institute in 1927, which included Jacques Abram and the older Cuban, Jorge Bolet.

So mother Anna sought and found financial backing for Sidney to enable him to attend the Curtis Institute which at that time charged tuition. Several individuals, patrons of the arts in Miami, contributed to his Conservatory expenses. Mrs. Cohen and Mr. W. F. Miller, president of the Miller-Dunn Company in Miami, Florida, were two individuals who gave him scholarship funds. According to a Miami newspaper article, Sidney "received from the Miami Conservatory a ten-year scholarship for *any* conservatory he might choose to attend that would include conservatory tuition, tutoring, and living expenses."

At Curtis, these enrollees attended the same classes in music and languages. They lived in the same rooming house within walking distance of the Curtis Institute. For those child prodigies, the advanced studies included music theory, *solfège*, and English literature. Years later, when Sidney Foster, the Indiana University professor, recounted to our Sunday afternoon piano class, he described English class with their teacher, Miss Mary Berne, who taught them Shakespeare's works, "To us, Shakespeare became our toys." We, his college students, were awestruck by that remark, as Shakespeare had not been in our grammar school books.

Originally Sidney's piano study in 1927 was to be with David Saperton, Hofmann's close associate. But on realizing the ten-year-old could barely read music, Saperton assigned him to Ms. Drummond for music reading study and to Vengerova for piano lessons. He explained to his Indiana University students (c. 1960) that:

> Vengerova was pedantically methodical. Even if we immediately understood the concept of the attack of dropping and shifting the weight of the arm on two notes, she insisted on keeping all of us on the same prescribed length of time—hers, before allowing us to proceed to the four-note unit, etc." He added, "All of us feared her, for she was quick to erupt if we displeased her by not doing what she thought she had made clear in our lesson. One frightful experience for me was of her histrionics that developed during a lesson on the Tchaikovsky barcarolle, *June*. When I obviously, though unintentionally, displeased her, her voice rose to a shrill pitch: 'No, no, no!' as she stood up over my music, which

she slashed over and over with a pencil. I became frightened, so I stood up and ran toward the studio door, at which time she rolled up my music and hurled it towards me. But an hour later when I walked in the Curtis corridors she appeared, having left her studio, and sweetly greeted me with 'Hello, Sidney,' as though the earlier drama had not occurred.

But regardless of the distasteful episodes of some lessons, Sidney loved playing the piano and composing. The memory of positive attention and recognition his playing received in Miami from trusted professionals helped him cope during his first period away from his family. The 'ups and downs' at Curtis, though hurtful, did not, however, prepare him or his family for his dismissal from the Institute before the end of his third year in 1929. According to hearsay, two individuals in the administrative offices of Curtis had been embezzling funds from Sidney's Miami sponsors. In anticipation of discovery they summoned the twelve-year-old and informed him that he was being dismissed because "You've been a bad boy." His recalling of that painful episode from his childhood was one I personally heard while I attended graduate school at Indiana University. He spoke of the train ride home from Philadelphia escorted by these two men. How this duo fared with the astute and loving mother Anna when she listened to their contrived mendacity was something he did not mention. What is known is that those two individuals were fired from their Curtis jobs once all the details were uncovered.

The end of this saga played itself out years later when, as a college applicant to Juilliard, Sidney Foster was told by the Juilliard admissions in 1934 that he could not be accepted because of his past Curtis record. That hitherto long-forgotten episode, having resurfaced, had to be addressed. So, Sidney Foster contacted the Curtis authorities because some time earlier he had learned of the particulars of the embezzling and the subsequent dismissal of the two men responsible for it. But now he was confronting the fact that the records at Curtis had to be cleared so he could be accepted at Juilliard. His inquiry in 1934 pushed the Curtis into action on his behalf to right old wrongs. An invitation was extended for him to return to Curtis—contrary to the usual policy of Curtis not to re-admit students who had left or had been dismissed. Sidney Foster returned to Curtis as a young man and four years later earned the coveted Artist's Diploma in 1938.

In 1940 after he won the Leventritt Competition, publicity about his background meant 'having to save face' by putting out an old dog's story, possibly with some truth, but however cute, was somewhat contrived. The November 5, 1941, Carnegie Hall program of his solo recital debut makes reference to it:

At the famous musical Institute, he was regarded as a young rebel, it being his habit to attend classes with his puppy in tow and other such unconventional practices. The authorities asked him to leave.

But that Carnegie Hall debut performance of 1941 was just the beginning of Sidney Foster's concert career. Many more concert performances in this most prestigious of American concert halls and in other beautiful venues would follow.

Composer

Composing music for Sidney Foster was a spontaneous occurrence from the first time he touched the piano keys of the upright piano in his family's Florence, South Carolina, home. His father played the piano as a way to relax. But for Sidney, who had perfect pitch and phenomenal rhythmic sense, this upright was a means to express what was in his mind's ear. At first, he arranged songs he heard. Improvising music in different styles became a natural progression.

From age three until age nine, young Sidney played by ear. His first teacher, Earl Chester Smith, from the Conservatory of Music at the University of Miami, took on the formidable task to harness the fantastic natural talent without stifling or extinguishing young Sidney's originality. He had to teach him how to read music so he could notate what he composed.

After Josef Hofmann recommended that young Sidney apply for admission to the Curtis Institute of Music, Louis and Anna helped the ten-year-old plan for his enrollment to Curtis which called for filling out application forms. The application form asked the usual: name, instrument the student would be studying, personal information, parents' names, address, date of birth, and so forth. The eleventh question asked, "What is your purpose in studying music?" Young Sidney's answer was, "to become a composer." He knew what he wanted to become, and this application form of September 1, 1927, to the Curtis Institute asked, and the ten-year-old answered.

After beginning his classes at Curtis in 1927, he wrote a letter to his mother telling her that he was:

> writing a string quartet dedicated to Grandma and a Little *Fantasia* dedicated to (his brother) Edwin for him to play on his cello. I've written a piece dedicated to Miss Drummond and next I will write one for Miss Vosary (Miss

Drummond was a teacher at Curtis, and Miss Vosary taught in the Miami public schools).

During his second enrollment at Curtis as a college-age music major, he was in the music composition classes of the acerbic Professor Rosario Scalero (who had tenured appointments from 1924 to 1933 and from 1935 to 1946). As Sidney Foster related to his Indiana University piano class circa 1960:

> Scalero was impossible to please. Assignments were returned covered with unexplained red marks. Suspecting that pleasing this professor was 'not in the cards', one day he (Sidney Foster) approached Scalero and asked him, 'Professor, what is a good example of a Fugue, one that I can learn from?' Scalero opened his score to a Bach fugue and, 'point by point,' showed me why it was a superb fugue—elements missing in my 'red-ly' marked assignment. I thanked him and left his office with my Fugue. For my next assignment, I brazenly copied the Bach fugue *in my own manuscript* and waited with anticipation for its return. As I surmised, my hand-copied Bach fugue was returned, covered in red slashes. So I accepted the obvious message that *some* of these teachers at Curtis wanted to tell us that we weren't capable of doing well.

After graduating from Curtis in 1938, Sidney Foster composed, but only sporadically, as he was busy learning repertoire for competitions, performing in small chamber groups, and teaching privately. After winning the Leventritt Award in the fall of 1940, he was 'sidetracked' with the need to prepare for more regular concert appearances. However, a brilliant example of his composing efforts is the *Cadenza* he composed for the first movement of the Beethoven Third Piano Concerto played in his debut with the New York Philharmonic. It is a spectacular *Cadenza* (a copy of the *Cadenza* is to be found in Appendix C, where three of Foster's compositions have been included). When he played it, his bravura brought a thunderous ovation at the close of the first movement, delaying the continuation of the rest of the Concerto.

As he continued living in Manhattan throughout his twenties, his activities included playing yearly recitals in Carnegie Hall and chamber music trios in Town Hall with his newly formed flute, piano, and cello Trio with French flutist René LeRoy and cellist János Scholz, two European artists. The scarcity of literature for this specific instrumental combination encouraged Foster to commission trios from up and coming young composers like Bohuslav Martinů and Norman Dello Joio. In addition, two new works for this ensemble that were premièred in Town Hall were trios that Foster composed.

One of these Foster Trios was listed on the program as being written by a Panamanian composer, a certain Señor E. Silvera. The piece, entitled *Allende el Río* was described in the program notes to be a 'programmatic suite.' Perhaps Foster intended this to be a professional tactic, or maybe just as a joke.

Whatever the motivation, Foster chose not to take credit for its creation. As Bronja Foster tells it:

> Sidney arranged with a Latin American looking gentleman, a friend, to stand up and be recognized by the audience when the Trio was finished. The composer/critic Virgil Thomson was there and was most enthusiastic about this new work. His review stated that Mr. Silvera was a fine composer, reminiscent of Silvestre Revueltas, a much celebrated Mexican composer. Mr. Thomson rushed backstage to talk to the performers, wanting to see the score. After seeing it—the ink possibly still damp—he commented that the score was somewhat different from what he had heard. In addition, the name on the score was spelled differently than it was listed on the program.

Sidney Foster could improvise spontaneously, and he could create a convincing explanation as well. Be that as it may, this 1944 March 21 concert in Town Hall with the E. Silvera, aka Sidney Foster, trio would be followed for several more seasons with other performances by the very jovial ensemble of LeRoy, Foster, and Scholz.

Foster would compose sporadically—songs for colleagues, short cadenzas for isolated works, and re-writing of passages in works he felt could be made stronger. In 1955, he composed one rather charming duet for a narrator, a duet partner, his colleague Walter Robert, and him, using the text of James Thurber's *The Unicorn in the Garden*.

There were many who never knew Sidney Foster could compose. He always knew he wanted to. However, he was known mostly as a concert pianist. Composing was a creative facet of his complete musicianship that was very important to him, but life circumstances kept him from developing it fully.

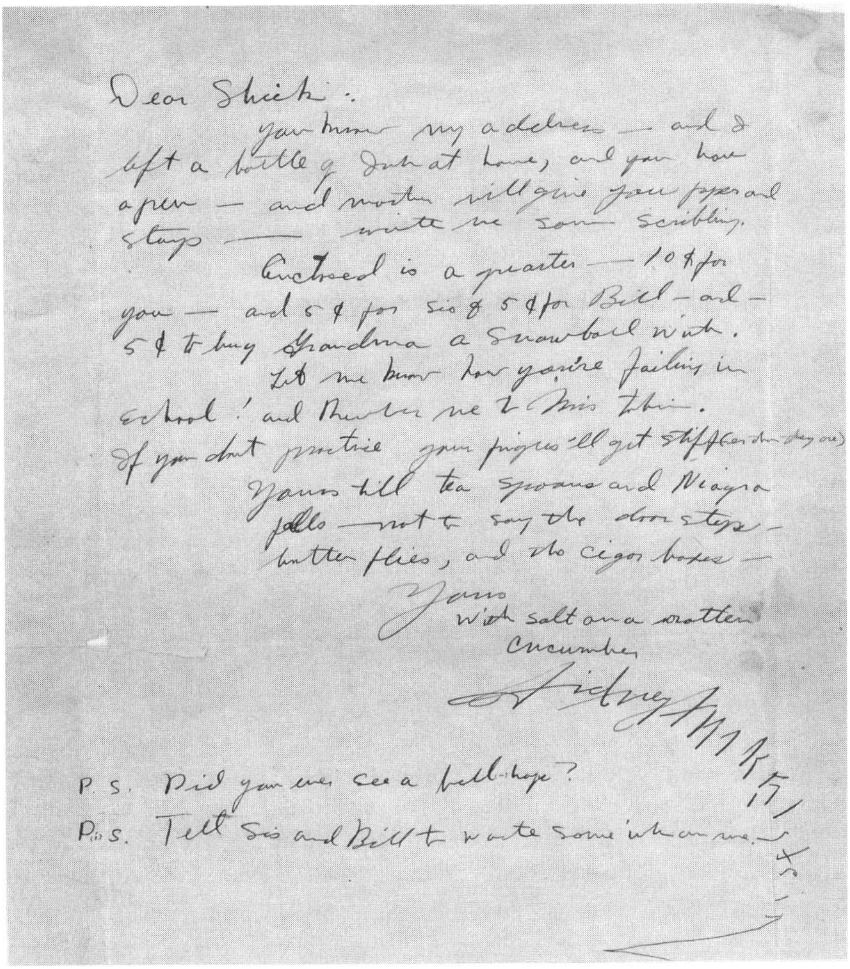

Figure 2.1. Letter written by Sidney to his brother, Edwin. Copyright Bronja S. Foster, all rights reserved.

The Leventritt

During his final year at Curtis, Sidney Foster was allowed to live away from Philadelphia. Commuting then from New York to Curtis became a weekly journey to complete the requirements for the Artist Diploma. Several other Curtis classmates including Jorge Bolet, Abbey Simon, Sol Kaplan, and Hershey Kay, who would become a music arranger for Leonard Bernstein, would also move to New York City where they quickly became a young, aspiring artistic colony that found energy from the City's cultural offerings. They were aware of each other's endeavors, and although they were sometimes competing for the same opportunities, they helped one another any way they could when the need arose: with food, a place to stay, taking messages, and so forth.

Nineteen thirty-nine was a memorable year for Sidney Foster. He won the MacDowell Competition which awarded him with a New York debut recital at the MacDowell Club, 166 East 73rd Street, on February 10, 1939. In late October, he married Curtis pianist classmate, Bronja Singer. Aside from the immediate family, the young couple enjoyed the unusually generous hospitality and friendship of the Oppenheimer family. Amy and Harry Oppenheimer, amateur musicians, would often invite them to their home where in the Oppenheimer music study, Sidney began learning the Johannes Brahms *Piano Concerto No. 2 in B-flat major, Op. 83*, which would be his Leventritt Competition piece.

Earlier in May 1940—months after Sidney and Bronja wed, they learned of the Leventritt Award, announced after the death of Edgar M. Leventritt, the prominent lawyer for the *New York Times*. In his will, Mr. Leventritt made the express provision for an annual competition for young musicians, to recognize and reward them, and that the competition would be in alternate years for pianists and violinists. Mr. Leventritt, aside from being an accomplished lawyer and a nephew to U.S. Supreme Court Justice David Leventritt, had been an enthusiastic amateur pianist and a member of *The Bohemians*, a musical organization committed to helping young performers.

At this time, the Leventritt Competition was only one of a handful of world-wide competitions for musicians. This first Leventritt was held in early October 1940. It was organized and directed by Mrs. Rosalie M. Leventritt. Her daughter, also named Rosalie J., and her husband, T. Roland Berner, eventually oversaw the Leventritt Foundation's finances.

Steinway Hall was the selected site for the preliminaries of this first Leventritt Competition, and thirty of the sixty applicants played there in that first round of the competition. From that group, nine played in the final hearings in Carnegie Hall which were heard on a Thursday, but the judges withheld the announcement of the winner until the following day. Each contestant had performed a concerto of his or her choice that was accompanied by a second

Figure 3.1. Edgar M. Leventritt. Permission supplied by Winifred B. Parker.

piano, and each played a solo piece. At that first Leventritt Competition, it was stipulated that contestants be between the ages of seventeen- and twenty-five-years old. They had to have lived in the United States, and they had to have performed publicly, but not with a major orchestra.

The judges at that time were Sir John Barbirolli, the then conductor of the New York Philharmonic, Arthur Judson, concert manager, Adolf Busch, violinist, and the pianists Rudolf Serkin and Nadia Reisenberg.

The prize consisted of a solo performance with the New York Philharmonic on the following March 16, 1941, in Carnegie Hall.

Although the twenty-three-year-old won the competition with the formidable B Flat Brahms Concerto, which he would have preferred to perform on his debut, it was the conductor who selected the entire program, including the soloist's concerto. Sir John Barbirolli had decided on the Ludwig van Beethoven First Concerto, but fortuitously, the winner, Sidney Foster, succeeded in pressing instead for the Beethoven *Piano Concerto No. 3 in C minor, Op. 37*, certainly a more substantial debut piece. To further enhance that opportunity, Foster composed that virtuoso cadenza for the first movement that he played spectacularly and which occasioned an extraordinary spontaneous prolonged ovation from the audience, postponing the continuation of

Figure 3.2. Sidney Foster, American pianist, made his debut Sunday with the New York Philharmonic at Carnegie Hall. Chatting with him during intermission, left to right, are Jacques Singer Foster, Bronja Foster, and John Barbirolli, the orchestra director. Associated Press.

the Concerto. The following day, several New York City newspapers wrote about the Leventritt debut. Headlines ranged from the whimsical "TWO FOR THE MONEY WITH SPAGHETTI ON THE SIDE" (Henry Simon of the *PM Daily*) to the most ecstatic pronouncement from the *New York Times*' writer Noel Straus: *"OVATION TO FOSTER"* . . . *"Brilliant! A richly gifted performer."* The foresight and generosity of Edgar M. Leventritt was a major statement that generated an artistic energy and movement in the United States, establishing America as a viable leader in the artistic world. Winning the Leventritt Award was the singularly most defining event that catapulted the beginning of a concert career for Sidney Foster.

After the Leventritt: LeRoy-Foster-Scholz Trio

In the New York concert season of 1941-42, Sidney Foster became a founding member of a unique chamber music ensemble consisting of flute, piano, and cello, with French flutist René LeRoy, and Hungarian cellist János Scholz. In the previous season, and with his highly successful debut with the New York Philharmonic—the award for winning the first Leventritt Competition—Mr. Foster became a current concert commodity. His management encouraged and promoted his participation in chamber music, especially with René LeRoy, who was a glamorous newcomer to the concert scene.

This instrumental combination was a challenge to performers since the repertoire for flute, piano, and cello was sparse. While the 1775 Boieldieu *Piano Trio, Op. 5* was known, as was the Weber *Trio in G minor, Op. 63*, both were infrequently heard, and their scores languished on music shelves. The instrumental combination of this new trio was a fresh idea. The time and challenge to performers to promote such a new ensemble and to develop new repertoire that would pique the audience's curiosity had arrived.

The LeRoy-Foster-Scholz Trio proved to be a most effective ensemble. For half a dozen seasons, it offered concerts in Town Hall performing older original works, arrangements of ballet music made especially for their ensemble, and most importantly the members' commissioned trios from living composers such as Norman Dello Joio and Bohuslav Martinů, whose works since have become part of the chamber music repertoire during these past six decades.

That opportunity was also one for the composer-talents of Sidney Foster to explore. Two of the trios that he composed for his flute, piano, cello ensemble were heard numerous times and were critically well received. Unfortunately, the scores were never submitted for publication, and they have been lost. To set the record straight: although the trios by Norman Dello Joio and Bohuslav Martinů were commissioned and dedicated to the LeRoy-Foster-Scholz Trio, the published scores do not acknowledge that fact. However, the program notes from the Town Hall concerts do and the critics also mention the première performances as commissioned works in their concert reviews.

A historic perspective concerning this ensemble of musicians is that, because of the horrible years of World War II, many individuals who could escape Europe found their way to America. René LeRoy was one of those musicians who came to New York and was extremely active and successful while he was in the States. However, with the war's end, Leroy, as well as many others, returned to their native countries. Thus, LeRoy's time with the LeRoy-Foster-Scholz Trio was brought to an end. In Europe, his career and life were renewed most happily and brilliantly as both performer and teacher. He died in Paris on January 3, 1985, seven years after Sidney Foster's death. Below are two selected programs performed at the Town Hall in New York City:

THE TOWN HALL SEASON 1943-44
WEDNESDAY EVENING MARCH 1, 1944

Trio in D major: Josef Haydn
  Allegro / Allegretto / Presto

Sonata da Camera: Gabriel Pierné
  Prélude / Sarabande / Finale

Trio for Flute, Cello and Piano (First performance): Norman Dello Joio
  Moderato / Adagio / Allegro con brio

La Boîte à Joujoux: Dohnányi/R. Casadesus

Allende el Río (First performance in New York): E. Silvera*
  Feria en la plaza / La niña del alcalde / Añoranza pastoral
  La iglesia Santa Anna / Matrimonio pueblano

There was no composer E. Silvera. Allende el Río was composed by Sidney Foster

THE TOWN HALL SEASON 1944-45
WEDNESDAY, FEBRUARY 28, 1945

Trio in D major, Op. 5: François Boieldieu
  Allegro / Larghetto / Allegro vivace

Figure 4.1. René LeRoy, Sidney Foster, János Scholz in 1945. Foster family collection.

Trio in G minor: Carl Maria von Weber
  Allegro / Scherzo / Andante arioso / Allegro

Trio in F major (Première performance): Bohuslav Martinů
  Allegro ma non troppo / Andante / Finale-Allegro

Trio: Norman Dello Joio
  Allegro / Adagio spiritoso

Trio (First performance): Sidney Foster
  Allegro / Dirge / Rondo

Sidney Foster and Norman Dello Joio

The chance meeting of Sidney Foster and Norman Dello Joio in 1943 was indeed serendipitous! Just two years before they met, Sidney Foster had won the first Leventritt Award which immediately gave him a high profile reputation in New York. Audiences and critics had begun following his career, paying attention to how and *what* he played. Foster was one who relished promoting individuals and their artistic ideas. And on a personal note, meeting Dello Joio revived his love for composing and interpreting new works.

Their first meeting is 'story book' and charming. In a September 2003 interview this writer had with Mr. Dello Joio at his home in East Hampton, New York, Dello Joio recalled:

During a sudden downpour in Manhattan in early February of 1943, we collided with our umbrellas at the doorway of the Carnegie Tavern. After uttering the initial amenities, we discovered that we were both musicians. Foster spoke of his upcoming Carnegie Hall recital on the first of March. I asked what works he was to play, and he mentioned Bach, Beethoven, Chopin, and Debussy." I asked him, "What contemporary American music was he going to perform?" Foster replied, "None." I asked "Why not?" Foster's response was, "Because there isn't any." I objected strongly, "Yes, there is!" to which Foster asked, "What?" "My Sonata," I retorted! "I haven't heard of it," Foster replied.

After the rain and their refreshment, the pair went to Dello Joio's apartment, where he played a movement of his First Sonata for Foster. After hearing it, Sidney said that he liked it and asked to hear the rest of it. "I haven't composed it yet," said Dello Joio. Typically, the fast-learner Foster told the composer, "Finish it, and I will première it on my Carnegie Hall concert in three weeks."

True to his word, on Monday evening March 1, 1943, in Carnegie Hall, Sidney Foster introduced Norman Dello Joio formally to the world for the first time in as prestigious a venue as any unknown young composer could dream of. Without a doubt, Foster's actions hastened Norman Dello Joio's public career with that première of his *Sonata for Piano, No. 1,* in Carnegie Hall.

The Dello Joio *Sonata for Piano, No. 1,* appeared after intermission. The program stated that it was a world première performance. During my interview with Mr. Dello Joio, I asked him about that night and how he felt about being featured alongside Bach, Beethoven, and Chopin. He told me candidly:

I was so nervous and excited with the fact that my music was being performed in a place where so many famous people had been heard before *me* that I cannot tell you how Sidney played or how my music was received. But afterwards, I asked my mother who had attended, what she thought of the fact that my piece had been played in Carnegie Hall. And she said: 'It's just fine, Norman.' When I continued to press her about it, she finally added: 'It was just fine, Norman; but I just wish you could play the piano as beautifully as Sidney!'

Years later when I was a student at Indiana University, Mr. Foster confided that the movement that Norman played for him that rainy night when they met would become the *last* movement of the First Sonata. The published score bears the dedication: "To Sidney Foster, in friendship and admiration." This work, published by Hargail Music Press, is edited by Sidney Foster. The dates February 1-4, 1943, appear at the end of the score.

After this Carnegie Hall performance in 1943, the Foster/Dello Joio professional and personal friendship continued. That same year Foster became a founding *member* and the promoter of the Flute/Cello/Piano ensemble with flutist René LeRoy, and cellist János Scholz. This new development gave Foster the idea to commission a trio from his friend, Norman, which he did. The Dello Joio *Trio for Flute, Cello, and Piano* was premièred in Town Hall on March 1, 1944, a year to the day after Foster's debut of the Dello Joio *Sonata for Piano, No. 1.* Stunningly, just the month before, on February 1, 1944, Sidney Foster had premièred Dello Joio's *Sonata for Piano, No. 2!*

Again at Carnegie Hall, the second Dello Joio Sonata was billed as a world première. It appeared after intermission following the Beethoven Waldstein Sonata. As the 1944-45 concert season began in Carnegie Hall, once more Sidney Foster would tell Manhattan to *"listen to our own American music."* So Foster played the world première of Dello Joio's *Prelude to a Young Musician* on his Carnegie Hall concert that October 18, 1944. For Dello Joio, as the song states, 1944 "was a very good year." Three of his works were premièred in world class venues!

In 1952, the Foster family moved to Bloomington, Indiana. Sidney continued to promote his friend's music. That April 27, 1952, Foster introduced Dello Joio's *Sonata for Piano, No. 3*, to a most enthusiastic Indiana University crowd. By then, Dello Joio had become well-known and had established himself as one of America's leading young composers. Unquestionably, Foster's early performances of Dello Joio's works had opened doors for him, encouraging a more careful consideration of his music.

At that time Indiana University had been gaining international prestige, and Sidney Foster had become a driving force who attracted exceptional student talent. Characteristically, Foster had not forgotten about his friend. On May 12, 1955, Foster became instrumental in staging a special concert tribute to honor Norman Dello Joio. The 'Belles of Indiana', a women's choral ensemble, presented Dello Joio's *A Jubilant Song*. The following nights of May 13 and 14, the Indiana University opera department produced the world première of his opera, *The Ruby*.

Throughout his teaching and concert career, Sidney Foster continued to champion his friend's music. On November 16, 1964, while on a much celebrated concert tour in Russia, he played Dello Joio along with Mozart, Beethoven, and Prokofiev in Moscow and later in several other Russian cities in the most prominent of Russian concert halls.

In his 90-some-odd years, Norman Dello Joio composed hundreds of works, several commissions that have garnered prizes, including the Guggenheim Fellowship, the New York Music Critics Circle Award, an Emmy and the Pulitzer Prize for his string orchestra piece *Meditations on Ecclesiastes*. But before he earned all of this fame, Dello Joio had walked about Manhattan like hundreds of other gifted composers until that first important break—his debut that his newly-found friend provided in Carnegie Hall on March 1, 1943.

Dello Joio acknowledged in our 2003 interview that "Sidney was a very generous individual. We had a great friendship, and although we saw each other infrequently because of our separate professional lives, we kept in touch, and we were appreciative of each other's accomplishments."

He added that Mrs. Foster had called him in late January of 1977 to say, "Sidney would like to see you, Norman." At that time Dello Joio was the Dean of the Fine and Applied Arts School at Boston University, and Sidney Foster was a patient in a Boston Hospital. Dello Joio had not known of Foster's illness or of his presence in Boston to receive medical care. It is most significant that Sidney asked to see his friend that fateful day. The visit was a farewell, an *addio* for the two longtime friends. Sidney Foster died a few days later on Monday, February 7, 1977.

Figure 5.1. Norman Dello Joio and Sidney Foster discussing the Dello Joio's Piano Sonata. James Abresch, 200 W. 57th St. NY, NY (as marked on 1940s photo). Foster family collection.

Stages Where Sidney Foster Walked

The first time I heard a Sidney Foster public performance was in Corpus Christi, Texas, at the Del Mar College Auditorium. Mr. Foster was a handsome, dark-haired man in his mid-thirties who had been entertaining audiences since he was three-years-old in his first concert venue: his own living room in Florence, South Carolina. From that 'homey, modest stage,' he progressed to public recitals in Miami and New Orleans, the towns to where his family moved. His early piano teachers 'showed him off' frequently in their studio recitals and in local competitions. At the Curtis Institute of Music where he enrolled in 1927, he played in the Curtis studios and in student recitals.

A decade later, after winning the MacDowell Club Award in 1938, he made his debut performance in a prestigious venue for young professionals— The MacDowell Club. Following that success, Sidney Foster won the First Leventritt Competition in late 1940 which gave him a walk on the boards of Carnegie Hall and his orchestral debut.

Throughout his twenties, his life in Manhattan was a series of performances that acquainted him with many concert stages where other artists before him had played. He would yearly play solo recitals in Carnegie Hall; and, with his Flute/Piano/Cello Trio, he would return to Town Hall where the ensemble played for several seasons. At the Lewisohn Stadium in July 1942, audiences cheered after he played the Tchaikovsky Concerto with Richard Korn, former assistant conductor of the National Orchestral Association, conducting the New York Philharmonic. At the Potomac Watergate, another outdoor amphitheater, another record-breaking crowd received his performance with wild enthusiasm.

In the old Metropolitan Opera House, circa 1944, he joined a visiting Russian Ballet company to perform the *Paganini Ballet*—choreographed

Figure 6.1. Sidney Foster and Jorge Bolet in Amsterdam. Uncredited. Foster family collection.

by Michel Fokine—and danced to the music of Sergei Rachmaninoff. After playing some eighteen solo recitals and concerto performances in Carnegie Hall, Sidney Foster began playing in the Alice Tully Hall of the new Lincoln Center for the Performing Arts in the 1970's.

The acclaim Foster received was for the most part, found in the critics' statements, extravagant praise. In quoting the *New York Sun*'s review of 1947 when Foster was just thirty-years-old, the following is stated: "One need no longer add the qualifying phrase 'of our younger pianists,' for, though he is still of this description, his attainments are on a level with those of our most eminent mature musicians." Walter Damrosch, who was considered 'the venerable dean of American music,' upon hearing Foster for the first time in New York in the Russian Ballet Company's production previously mentioned, declared: "Young as he is, he already ranks with the foremost pianists that have visited us (in the USA) from European countries."

Foster played in many American cities and in Europe, Russia, and Asia, in some of the most renowned concert halls. But a very unusual venue, most likely not tried out by most artists, was his playing in a penal institution. Sidney Foster played a full-length recital in the State Penitentiary in Cañon,

Figure 6.2. Sidney Foster with inmates at State Penitentiary in Cañon, Colorado. Karol Smith, photographer (as stamped on 1940s photo). Foster family collection.

Colorado. He became the first established concert artist to do so, and he became interested in the problems of the moral rehabilitation of law breakers that, after that recital, he began organizing a committee of some of his distinguished colleagues to volunteer for more of these concerts.

Evolution of Programming

The essence of Sidney Foster's musicianship can be gleaned through the concert seasons as he developed recital programs. Those professional solo recitals began with his Town Hall debut on February 10, 1939—the prize for winning the MacDowell Club Award that year. It is an ambitious program that represents eight composers including a work by David Saperton, his teacher, sufficient variety, but only one major work—the Op. 110 Beethoven Sonata.

I

Organ Prelude and Fugue in D major, *Bach-Philippe*
Sonata in A-flat major, Op. 110, *Beethoven*

II

Ballade in D major, Op. 10, No. 2, *Brahms*
Ballade in B minor, Op. 10, No. 3, *Brahms*
Moto Perpetuo, *Weber*

Polonaise in C minor, Op. 40, No. 2, *Chopin*
Valse in A-flat major, Op. 34, No. 1
Barcarolle in F sharp major, Op. 60

III

Poisson D'or, *Debussy*
La terrasse des audiences du clair de lune
La fille aux cheveux de lin

Zephyr, *Saperton*
Valse aus der Ballet Naila, *Delibes-Dohnányi*

The solo recitals we play as students are for the most part designed by our private piano teachers. Their major considerations are the inclusion of the accepted style periods, multiple movement works such as sonatas or suites, a variety of smaller works, and an appropriate 'ender upper' which is generally brilliant with a *fortissimo* finish. When we are 'out on our own,' however, it is up to us to build our own programs, and these are determined by our taste and what is in our repertoire.

Foster's Carnegie Hall recital on November 5, 1941, after he won the Leventritt Award and played his orchestral debut earlier on March 17, 1941—like the Town Hall debut program, presents many (seven) different composers—, but that time there are two major works: the Franck *Prélude, Chorale et Fugue*, and the Schumann *Carnaval, Op. 9*.

NOVEMBER 5, 1941,
CARNEGIE HALL

Franck: Prélude, Chorale et Fugue
Schumann: Carnaval, Op.9

Chopin: Nocturne in F major, Op. 15, No. 1
   Etude, Op. 10, No.4, C-sharp minor
   Etude, Op. 10, No. 9, F minor
   Etude, Op. 10, No. 5, G-flat major
   Etude, Op. 10, No. 6, E-flat minor
   Etude, Op 10, No. 8, F major

Turina: Danzas, Op. 55, Nos. 2 and 5
Shostakovich: Polka from the *Golden Age*
Debussy: Prelude—*La terrasse des audiences*
David Guion: The Harmonica Player
Delibes (Dohnányi: Naila Waltz

From his earliest endeavors as a 'programmer' of music, Sidney Foster, the child, understood that there were different styles of music. Sometimes when he improvised, he would ask his audience what they would like to hear, "some Spanish music? Indian? Older Classical?...." and he would improvise spontaneously different pieces. Dottie, his sister, recalls that sometimes a member of the family would have to poke him from behind the curtain to let him know the piece had gone on long enough.

After his formal study at Curtis and with experience, there was a distinct evolution and development in Foster's recital programming, as he added to his repertoire. The changes with each season's offerings reflect growth, and exceptional intellect. That pianist was not just a mere technical acrobat. This is not to dismiss his phenomenal technique—clarity in speed, titanic power, always a big beautiful tone, and trills—WOW!

Foster developed three basic types of program architecture:

1. Variety encompassing several, even many composers, including at least two important multi-movement works, and a variety of shorter pieces by different composers. He played this type of programming frequently.
2. Comparing or contrasting of two composers. This was a very elegant and provocative type, evident in his middle years, and one that he developed on his own.
3. Occasionally an all-sonata recital.
4. A return to the variety type at the end of his career as well as a change of venues, from Carnegie Hall to the Lincoln Center's Alice Tully Hall.

Examples of his programs that contrasted two composers reveal an architecture of the works and their composers in a somewhat mirror design. The outer pieces, first and last ones, are shorter in length, but of course, very different. The opening is a lyrical Chopin *Prelude, Op. 45*, and the finale is a virtuoso Prokofiev *Toccata*. The pieces before and after intermission are the multi-movement works—the brilliant Frédéric Chopin *Sonata* prepares the audience for the intermission:

Prelude in C-sharp minor, Op. 45, *Chopin*
Barcarolle, Op. 60
Sonata in B minor, Op. 58

Allegro maestoso
Presto
Largo
Finale—Allegro assai

INTERMISSION

Sonata No. 9 in C major, Op. 103, *Prokofiev*

Allegretto
Scherzo—Allegro vivace
Andante
Allegro

Eight Vision Fugitives, Op. 22
Toccata, Op. 11

With a slight variation of the 1961 recital model, Foster contrasts Mendelssohn and Brahms in 1965, another example of the mirroring of composers.

Mendelssohn: Fantasy, Op. 28
Brahms: Sonata, Op. 5

INTERMISSION

Brahms: Four Ballades, Op. 10
Mendelssohn: Three Etudes, Op. 104

One all-sonata program that he played in Tampa, Florida, in October of 1967, presented the Mozart *Sonata in G major, K. 283*; the Brahms *Sonata in F minor, Op. 5;* the Rachmaninoff *Sonata in B-flat minor, Op.36;* and the Prokofiev *Third Sonata in A minor*. The *St. Petersburg Times* critic, M. N. Shenk, headlined her review: "PIANIST FOSTER WALKS SLOWLY, BUT CARRIES A LARGE TALENT." She took note of his "serious countenance and subdued bearing . . . who became a virile, exciting and sensitive musician when he and his instrument joined forces. Foster is a thoroughly genuine musician."

At times he played all Romantic music programs, but single composer recitals were not his cup of tea. In the winter of 1959, having recovered from a major heart attack three years prior, Foster presented a come-back recital that revealed a completely cured and energized artist. His Bach English Suite in A minor displayed his affinity and understanding of Baroque style and an exquisite erudite interpretation of ornaments. His *Kreisleriana, Op. 16,* showed a rare understanding of Schumann. He received lavish praise in the *New York Times* . . . "glad to have him back . . . Excellent recital at Carnegie Hall. Sidney Foster played with the sort of insights when a man understands a work as a whole." The *New York Post* stated, "imagination, skill, and abandon . . . Sensitive performance, musicality and appealing lyricism." *Musical America* summed it up with "the piano sang again as it used to when the great masters of the past were at the keyboard."

CARNEGIE HALL
MONDAY EVENING, NOVEMBER 23 (1959)
AT 8:30 O'CLOCK

BACH: *English Suite in A minor*

II

SCHUMANN: *Kreisleriana*

INTERMISSION

III

BARTÓK: *Suite, Op. 14*
ALBÉNIZ: *Evocación*
PROKOFIEV: *Sonata, No. 3*

Sidney Foster's final New York recitals in 1970 and 1972 that he played in Alice Tully Hall were examples of his architectural variety, presenting seldom heard pieces, such as the Beethoven *Andante Favori*, the Hummel *La Bella Capricciosa*, and the marvelous Delibes-Dohnányi version of *Naila's Waltz* which was received ecstatically by the eager Julliard piano majors in the audience.

ALICE TULLY HALL CONCERT
FEBRUARY 1970

HUMMEL: *La Bella Capricciosa*
CHOPIN: *Ballade in F minor*
LISZT: *Sonata in B minor*
SCRIABIN: *Ninth Sonata*

MOSKOWSKI: *Au Guitarre*
PADEREWSKI: *Cracovienne Fantastique*
HOFMANN: *Berceuse*
DELIBES-DOHNÁNYI: *Naila's Waltz*

ALICE TULLY HALL
JANUARY 16, 1972
(FOSTER'S LAST NEW YORK RECITAL)

BEETHOVEN: *Andante in F*
Sonata, Op. 53 (the Waldstein)

LISZT: *Venice and Naples*
CHOPIN: *Barcarolle*

SCRIABIN: *Four Etudes, Op. 42*

PROKOFIEV: *Third Sonata in A minor*

The piano recital is an artistic event that Foster developed most brilliantly through the decades of his career. His programs were conceived with much thought and reflection about musical architecture and the relationship of style. He understood the elements that had to be considered for a satisfying program, much like a master chef plans a gourmet dinner.

Over the course of several decades, those programs reveal definite characteristics and ideas. Certain works like the Franck *Prélude, Chorale et Fugue* were favored by him, and on several programs would open the recital event. Most importantly, he was of the opinion that a fair evaluation by the listener of Foster's style in interpreting Mozart—especially a sonata—was to precede the Mozart with a contrasting style and composer. His Mozart was especially elegant.

His sense of a program became an amazing evolution. He had the requisite and obvious: his expressive and technical gifts, an immense repertoire, and a passion to perform. Through his programming, Sidney Foster became an extraordinary example to his students and his fellow artists. In his relatively short life, a span of just 59 years, he played 14 solo concerts and 3 concertos in Carnegie Hall. I was privileged to have heard him play two recitals in Carnegie Hall, and one of them within weeks of hearing two other great artists also in that Hall, Vladimir Horowitz and Emil Gilels. This gave me

Evolution of Programming 33

Figure 7.1. Walter Damrosch and Sidney Foster. Photographer Ben Greenhaus, 1475 Broadway, Times Building, (as marked on 1940s photo). Foster family collection.

the unique experience and basis for comparing pianists. According to Mrs. Sidney Foster (Bronja):

> Sidney loved to play in Carnegie Hall. He loved the sound and the ambience of the hall. For him, as with many other artists, Carnegie Hall had a presence, prestige, and the desired projection for music making. Undoubtedly, that concert hall served as an inspiration to him as he developed the architecture of his artistic events.

Orchestral Soloist

Winning the MacDowell Club Award (1939) and the first Leventritt Competition (1940) were the two timely events that got Sidney Foster's concert career started. The solo recital debut in the MacDowell Club Hall in 1939 (the MacDowell Prize) and his concerto performance with the New York Philharmonic in Carnegie Hall the following year, brought him the attention of well-established and powerful conductors such as Dimitri Mitropolous and Walter Damrosch. He signed a contract with the National Concert and Artists' Corporation (NCAC), and with his declaration to be a Steinway Artist, he was on his way.

The debut with the New York Philharmonic partnered him with Sir John Barbirolli on the Beethoven Third Piano Concerto in which he may very well have upstaged Sir John with his handsome freshness and his very own spectacular cadenza that he had composed for this occasion. It certainly did stop the Concerto with a sustained ovation after the first movement before allowing the Concerto to continue. Adding to that, the press releases that followed were unanimous in their praise.

Dimitri Mitropoulos and Foster re-interpreted the Beethoven Third Concerto again, ten years later in Carnegie Hall with the New York Philharmonic. A curious fact of that April 7, 1951, concert was Mitropoulos' inclusion of the Dello Joio orchestral work, *New York Profiles,* and the realization that this composer's first introduction in Carnegie Hall (Dello Joio's debut seven years earlier on March 1, 1943) was through Sidney Foster's brave and bold programming of his First Piano Sonata.

Just as Foster and Dello Joio became good friends, Mitropoulos would become a professional benefactor and collaborator with the pianist Foster, engaging him as soloist with the Minneapolis Symphony Orchestra on the Brahms B Flat Concerto, which they performed in Syracuse, New York, during a tour of that orchestra. Being a most generous individual, Mitropoulos extended to him the use of his New York apartment in the Great Northern Hotel, a place where Sidney Foster could practice without disruptions.

Foster's concerto repertoire was extensive, numbering over thirty works. He learned quickly. His interpretative instincts and stylistic sense were immediately on target, and excessive technical drills were unnecessary because of his extraordinary technical virtuosity.

Other conductors with whom he collaborated included William Steinberg with the Chicago Symphony Orchestra at Ravinia, Aaron Copland with the Boston Symphony Orchestra, Helmuth Froschauer with the Vienna Chamber Orchestra, Maurice Abravanel and the Utah Symphony Orchestra, Izler Solomon and the Indianapolis Symphony Orchestra, Jacques Singer and the Dallas Symphony Orchestra, and, on numerous Sunday broadcasts with the Radio City Music Hall Orchestra, with Hungarian conductor Erno Rapée, who had advised the young artist to change the name Finkelstein to the shorter surname: Foster, also adopted by all the living family.

The early concerto appearances with many other conductors which remain unnamed, replaced fantasy with the reality that being a concerto soloist is not always a satisfying experience. Much of the time the experience was most stressful as 'two equals'—conductor and soloist, more often than not—differed on critical matters such as *tempo* and expressive concepts which, furthermore, had to be worked out in minimum rehearsal time. Compromise is the key for a successful performance. I recall one of Mr. Foster's semi-humorous offhand quips, stating that "he'd followed most conductors."

Studying a concerto with him that he had performed brought about this mentor's great instruction, and as a bonus, his own recollections of his experience in learning and performing that particular work.

While studying the Rachmaninoff *Rhapsody on a Theme of Paganini* with Mr. Foster, I learned about Sol Hurok's role in bringing Russian ballet companies to the States in the 1940's. My ears were most stimulated by the ballet stories because my first paying job (one dollar an hour!) had been to play in the Ballet Studio of a dancer named Dolena, in my hometown of McAllen, Texas, who had been a former member of one of the Ballet Russe companies based in New York City.

The *Paganini Ballet*, based on the Paganini legend, was set to Rachmaninoff's then very new work, his *Rhapsody on a Theme of Paganini Op. 43*. In the summer of 1937, Rachmaninoff had visited with Michel Fokine at Senar, Rachmaninoff's home outside of Paris, and it had been Rachmaninoff's idea for Fokine to create choreography for this *Paganini Ballet*.

Antal Dorati conducted the première on June 30, 1939, at Covent Garden with Eric Harrison as piano soloist. Three years later, in December 1942,

Rachmaninoff himself performed the *Rhapsody* with Mitropoulos and the New York Philharmonic.

After Rachmaninoff's death in 1943, a Russian Ballet company returned to New York to perform the Fokine *Paganini Ballet*, but they did not bring a pianist. Antal Dorati again was to conduct this performance at the old Metropolitan Opera House in the 51st Street Theater. It became the task of Sol Hurok to find a pianist to perform this fairly new work with the visiting Russian ballet company.

After hunting unsuccessfully for someone who knew the piece, Foster's management persuaded him to learn the *Rhapsody on a Theme of Paganini*—which he did—in six days! According to reports of this performance, the piano was on a separate stage above the pit, to one side of the ballet dancers' stage. It had to have been a spectacular performance, as it prompted Walter Damrosch to rush backstage afterwards, past Dorati, inquiring, "Where is the pianist?"

In later concerto engagements, Sidney Foster performed in different venues including a date on July 31, 1947, at the Lewisohn Stadium with conductor Richard Korn, where the crowd responded with wild applause after hearing Foster's and Mr. Korn's rendition of the Tchaikovsky *Concerto No. 1 in B-flat minor for Piano and Orchestra, Op. 23.*

Aside from his own enjoyment as a performer, Sidney Foster was wholeheartedly committed to helping others in their efforts and pursuits of music making. A poignant episode that is telling of Foster's generous spirit occurred when on one snowy January day (1961) when young conducting students at Indiana University were presenting their exam-type of performances, one of the young conductors faced us, his audience, full of piano majors, and stated that his soloist had been snowbound in Indianapolis. "Would anyone in the audience volunteer to perform the first movement of the Grieg so that I may complete my semester's work?"

After a few moments passed and no one had volunteered, Sidney Foster graciously said he would. The young conductor was relieved, and we were treated to the professionalism and artistry—spur of the moment as it was—of Professor Foster! Let it snow! Let it snow!

The autumn of 1976 was a memorable one. Just months before he died, Foster learned the *Suite Fantastique, Op. 7,* by Ernest Schelling. This wonderful piece, though not in vogue, had not been heard since its composer had performed it in 1939.

Ernest Schelling was an American pianist/conductor who had developed one of the early series of children's concerts with the New York Philharmonic. Like Sidney Foster, Schelling composed sporadically because performing took priority.

Figure 8.1. Dimitri Mitropoulos. Susan Hoeller photos; 1 Sheridan Square, NYC. Foster family collection.

Today's artists should be performing this superb Romantic concerto monument by one of our early American composers. Mr. Foster played this Schelling piece in Dearborn, Michigan, with the Indianapolis Symphony Orchestra, conducted by Nat Gordon, and in Bloomington, Indiana, with the Bloomington Symphony Orchestra. With this revival of the *Op. 7*, unknowingly, Foster bid all of us his farewell.

Part Two

FOSTER'S PIANISM

Russian Roots, Russian Legacy

His Hands

His Piano Teachers

Where He Taught

The Pedagogue

Collaborator—Indiana University

The Concert Pianist and the Old World Scholar (An Unusual Partnership)

Architect of Piano Performance Doctorate

Russian Roots, Russian Legacy

In the late 19th century and throughout the 20th century, the aura and mystique of Russian superiority in music making—in pianism, on bowed instruments, and in the field of ballet music—can be justified. One only needs to recall the names of Anton Rubenstein, Alexander Scriabin, Leopold Godowsky, Sergei Rachmaninoff, and Joseph Lhevinne, to agree that the Russians and those who studied with those Russian teachers/musicians were great artists in what is considered the Russian tradition.

Sidney Foster's roots to the Russian school of pianism and music making are through his study with both David Saperton, who was greatly influenced by Leopold Godowsky, the extraordinary technician, and by Josef Hofmann—who was said to have been Anton Rubinstein's only private pupil—who singularly, as director of the Curtis Institute, admitted the ten-year-old to Curtis in 1927.

Aside from Foster's pianistic roots to Russian-trained musicians, his parents were of Russian and Polish backgrounds. His father and his family immigrated to the United States in the 1880's from Kiev; his mother's parents came from Poland. Coincidentally, Kiev was also the birthplace of Rosina Lhevinne and Solomon Stern, the artist/painter father of Isaac Stern. Those citizens who emigrated in the 1880's and early 1900's from Kiev considered themselves Russians, but they became voting citizens in their new homeland.

The spectacular technique that Foster possessed and his interpretive approach were in that 'grand manner' that is labeled the Russian school. His sound—regardless of what kind of piano he played—was phenomenally large. His use of the three pedals was not only for coloring, but for allowing him to free his fingers, as his concept was to 'use' the keys rather than to play them.

Although his lessons with the legendary Isabelle Vengerova, a former protégé of the Russian Annette Essipova, were at age ten through twelve, Foster explained that his technical approach incorporated, in part, some of Vengerova's ideas of transference of weight and relaxation.

Foster recounted to his Indiana University piano class that when he visited Mme. Vengerova long after he had established himself as a concert artist and teacher, their encounter was amicable. This was a contrast to her bitter reception towards him upon his reinstatement to the Curtis as a college student when he was not placed in the Vengerova piano studio, but in those of Josef Hofmann and David Saperton. In this friendly visit, Foster gratefully acknowledged to her the benefits and value of her ideas on technique and music, explaining and summarizing them, stating that he had incorporated them along with his own ideas in his teaching:

> She told me, in amazement, how accurately I had understood her method, even though I was just a child of ten when I studied with her and that many, many of her older students had failed to grasp her ideas as well as I had

His Hands

In considering hands that are perfect for piano playing, just as we think of tallness necessary for great basketball players, Sidney Foster's hands were perfect for projecting his musical talent. While the stout fingers looked as though they could not possibly move with speed, the nickname 'Sidney Faster,' given to him by Indiana University music students, fit him amazingly. Consider his recording of the Mendelssohn etudes and the Chopin *Etudes, Op. 10*—he recorded four of them—and you will hear what is meant by 'Sidney Faster.' The fat cushions of his fingertips, I believe, had a lot to do with the quality of the gorgeous crystalline tone he produced at the instrument, be it in Mozart, Schumann, Chopin, Prokofiev, or Rachmaninoff. His fingers, all four on each hand, were almost of the same length, and the palm was thick and cushiony. Together, these hands were directed by the concept in his mental ear and produced extraordinary power, poetry, and rhythmic precision.

One of his live performances I heard in April of 1965 in Boston was his rendition of the Bartók Third Piano Concerto with the Boston Symphony Orchestra conducted by Aaron Copland. His powerful sound rose above the orchestra's in the *fortissimo* climax of the third movement. This was an exceptional collaboration which the orchestra's musicians acknowledged with their ovation to him at the close of the piece. Music making of this caliber, and with only one hour of rehearsal time, is rare.

Foster was of slight stature, probably stood at five feet six inches tall, and most of his life his weight hovered at 135 pounds. Meaningless gestures were not in his style or approach. When he sat at the piano, it was economy of motion and none of the facial or body English you see in the likes of many younger players of yesteryears and today as well. He was a fast learner, not only of the notes but of the music concept within the composer's notation.

Sidney Foster believed that the artist's job was to search the score before him and to determine what the composer had intended, the concept encoded in the notes. Foster was critical of those who approached the music with the attitude "What can I do to it?" As he put it succinctly in the former approach—the former is the wheels the composer's work rides on, while the latter, the musical work becomes the wheels with which the musical player shows off.

On days when he practiced, the most time he spent in practice time was two hours and sometimes less than two hours considering committee meetings, recitals and concerts he attended for colleagues and students. Eight hours of practice time for him was never needed or possible. In fact, he discouraged

Figure 10.1. Sidney Foster's hands. Photographs by Lincoln Foster.

his students from over-practicing, lest these efforts become mindless and robot-like sessions.

What set Sidney Foster apart from other musician-mentors were his interpretations of our piano monuments. Especially and notably, the element of *rubato*—or his concept of it—was extraordinary. We hear about good *rubato* vs. rhythmic distortion as when a pianist holds or lingers on one or two notes that interrupt the flow of the music . . . all in the name of interpretation.

Rarely do I revisit a recording, as I will occasionally to an art museum to reexamine and take in the beauty of a painting. I do just that with the two CD set, *Ovation to Sidney Foster* (IPAM 1204), the technically unedited album of his live performances put together by some of his students as a tribute after his death. I listen to the seventeenth cut of the first CD, the Godowsky *Alt Wien*. It is without a doubt the essence of what *rubato* should be . . . delicate, elastic and subtle. It is a perfect jewel without equal. One hears all the requisites in this interpretation: a big gorgeous tone, an expressive scale of dynamic colors, spontaneity, and that subtle rhythmic expansion of all its elements. *Alt Wien*, the last piece on the first CD, is a special miniature, fortunately captured in a live performance.

His Piano Teachers

In Florence, South Carolina, Sidney Foster's piano playing was guided by his phenomenal ear and natural talent. He did not read music. When his family moved to Miami in 1925, however, Earl Chester Smith, the head of piano studies at the Conservatory of Music at the University of Miami, became his first teacher. It was in this school and through this teacher's efforts that the child Sidney began learning to read and notate the music he composed. It was also in Miami that Josef Hofmann 'discovered' young Sidney and recommended that he enroll at Curtis. There, Isabelle Vengerova thus became his second piano teacher in 1927.

After the strange series of episodes involving the financial manipulation of Sidney's scholarship funds and his dismissal from Curtis in 1930, he returned to his family who now resided in New Orleans, Louisiana. At that time he enrolled in the piano department at the Newcomb School of Music as a student of Walter Goldstein, who became his third teacher and most dedicated advocate. In New Orleans, Sidney also had a few lessons with Arthur Newstead.

During those years, 1930 to 1934, as Goldstein's student, Sidney flourished. He developed technically, musically, and he added to his piano repertoire. Goldstein also taught him classes in harmony and entered him in several area competitions which Sidney won, including one that awarded the thirteen-year-old the prize of a Wurlitzer grand piano. The *New Orleans Morning Tribune* was one of the sponsors of the competition where over 650 young pianists entered.

At the beginning of his senior year in high school, Sidney spent two months taking lessons with Winfred Molkin in Boston, but he returned to New Orleans to finish his senior year in school and to study with Walter Goldstein.

Where He Taught

Sidney Foster's first private piano studio was in New Orleans. He was just fifteen living at home with his parents. Fortuitously, he had a grand piano to teach on—the prize that he had won at age thirteen! Teaching was a natural progression from studying and performing, and he enjoyed it. Two years later when he re-enrolled as a first year college-age student at Curtis, he continued teaching privately. Teaching provided some financial means, and most significantly, it was the beginning of developing his ideas for teaching the instrument and its literature.

From the start, Foster was thoughtful about how he played the piano. He had had two piano teachers who were conservatory professors in Miami and New Orleans before his time with Isabelle Vengerova at Curtis. He absorbed her technical method which espoused the idea of using hand weight to navigate the keyboard. To this, Foster discovered the difference in the use of arm weight when the music passage called for it with the lighter touch of only hand weight. So, in studying with him, we learned that there are two ways to let that arm weight hang as we played the keys: all the way down, which gives us great power; and up slightly with mostly weight from the hands, that enables greater speed for those passages that call for it.

In 1937, with few requirements remaining for the completion of his Artist Diploma at Curtis, Sidney Foster moved to New York to live with his recently widowed mother. He commuted to Philadelphia weekly by train, and his weeks were filled practicing and teaching a few students. He continued to teach privately in Manhattan for several years as he prepared, entered, and won the MacDowell and Leventritt Competitions.

In the summer of 1945, Sidney Foster got his first taste of employment in academe. That brief experience as a university teacher in Austin, Texas, was repeated four years later at Florida State University in Tallahassee, where he

48 *Where He Taught*

taught for two years. But after two years in the rigid academic atmosphere, he returned to New York where he resumed teaching privately.

At age thirty-four, Sidney Foster was in top form. With the end of the war, enrollments in colleges and universities increased dramatically, and universities began promoting their Schools of Music by developing formidable performance degree programs. That trend within the university systems encouraged the hiring of concert artists for their faculty in order to implement their new degree programs and the professionalism and standards of the concert world.

From the first time Wilfred C. Bain, Dean of Music at North Texas State University (currently The University of North Texas), heard the young Sidney Foster play with the Dallas Symphony Orchestra, he wanted to recruit Foster for his faculty. Those recruitment efforts continued until Wilfred C. Bain moved to Bloomington, Indiana, where he became the Dean of Music at Indiana University, and finally succeeded in persuading Sidney to join their ranks. In February 1952, Foster and Bain worked out a contractual agreement that would permit him to continue concertizing while under contract to teach. Dean Bain was most accommodating because of his determination to

Figure 12.1. Abbey Simon, Jorge Bolet, David Saperton, and Sidney Foster. Whitestone Photo, 124 W. 72nd St., NY 23, NY (#5543-20, photo number). Late 1960s or early mid-70s. Foster family collection.

establish a university School of Music that stressed performing, not just the granting of academic degrees.

Throughout his tenure at Indiana University, Foster continued concertizing, playing yearly in Carnegie Hall, and eventually in the Alice Tully Hall of the Lincoln Center for the Performing Arts in New York. His concert work contributed to his reputation, and he became a highly sought-after teacher. He enjoyed attracting piano students from all corners of the world.

He was in demand as well for presenting workshops and master classes to music teachers in different locales, some of which were referrals of former students. Then there were piano competitions that he adjudicated which had him coming full circle from winner to judging the new generation of winners.

Though Sidney Foster's early ambition to become a composer was derailed after winning the Leventritt Award, serendipitously this change of course started him on a very special life's journey to impart and share with his students what he had learned about the art of piano playing and music making. In teaching, he coaxed indirectly those of us who studied with him to do the

Figure 12.2. A post-concert reception for Van Cliburn by Indiana University piano faculty: (L to R) Abbey Simon, Sidney Foster, Van Cliburn, Alfonso Montecino and Josef Battista: April 1964. Photograph courtesy of the *Bloomington Herald Times*.

same . . . that is, to pass on that which we had learned from others, adding, of course, our own enriching enhancements.

At Indiana University, his influence was felt positively as he persuaded other artists like Abbey Simon, Jorge Bolet, and Menahem Pressler to join him on the faculty. That was the place and the time to share their knowledge with the future generations of artists. He became one of the architects of the Performance Doctorate degree. More importantly, he continued to demonstrate by performing. He was an early pioneer in the trend for artists to affirm that those who can, can also teach!

The Pedagogue

Sidney Foster began teaching private piano lessons in New Orleans when he was fifteen. This was the time when he himself was also learning the literature and acquiring the skills to notate what he composed. Throughout his graduate-student years at Curtis, past his graduation and his move to New York City, Foster continued teaching privately.

The early years in New York City from 1938 to 1945 were most productive and extraordinary. Foster won the MacDowell and the Leventritt competitions; he married his Curtis classmate Bronja Singer; taught privately; and, all the while he was augmenting his concert repertoire. He played solo recitals and chamber music concerts with the LeRoy, Foster, Scholz Trio, for which he also composed a few works.

His first experience teaching in a university was at the University of Texas in Austin as a summer session faculty replacement for the ailing Dalies Frantz. He was a mere twenty-eight-year old, ten years younger than Frantz, but the important consideration for Dean E. William Doty, who hired Foster, was that he was a Leventritt winner who would teach and perform. And after he played a concert in Austin two weeks before the end of summer school, a very prominent gentleman and local piano teacher who was twice Foster's age immediately went to Dean Doty and asked to be assigned to Foster's studio for lessons. Though he was uncomfortable in taking this gentleman as a student, Foster met him in his studio to hear him. The gentleman explained:

> Well, I'm frustrated. I can't play anything for more than 30 or 40 seconds if it is running notes, as I quickly tire. I stop and start again. I've studied with several very important people, but I have normal hands, and I have little strength.

This gentleman who came for lessons with Sidney Foster was Mr. Irl Allison, who was the founder of the highly successful and worthy *Piano Guild of Texas*—the yearly auditions—and eventually the highly successful *National Guild of Piano Teachers*. Foster told of the encounter with his summer session student as follows:

> For the two weeks he studied with me, that end of summer, he came daily for about ten or fifteen minutes every day. I showed him how to practice Hanon and how to apply that to Czerny, and how, therefore, he would apply those physical principles to the Chopin etudes.

At his first lesson, Mr. Allison had played a few measures of a Chopin etude, stopped, and Foster said, "Go on." And he said, "I will, but I have to rest." "He played very stiffly." Mr. Allison worked with Sidney Foster a sum of twelve short lessons that summer. However, knowing that Sidney Foster would be back to play in San Antonio, Texas, two months later, he had Mr. Foster promise to "give him a lesson when he was in San Antonio and check up on what he had been doing." Foster promised to hear him in two months, which he did. At that lesson in San Antonio, Irl Allison played the Chopin 'Winter Wind' Etude. But before playing it, he told Foster, "I don't want you to interrupt me if I play it a second time without stopping, or even a third time." According to Sidney Foster, Irl Allison sat down and played the 'Winter Wind' Etude three times without stopping!—a remarkable feat, especially since Mr. Allison, a fifty-five-year-old man, had had to rest every few bars just two months before.

This proves that a teacher is only as good as his or her student. Mr. Allison faithfully tried every suggestion that Mr. Foster had given him, and he gained an endurance that he had never known or had before. More importantly, Mr. Allison knew it, and was grateful. Interestingly, some of the technical recommendations in the Piano Guild outlines are directly related to Irl Allison's study with Sidney Foster.

That was in Austin, Texas, in 1945. In the autumn of 1949, at Florida State University in Tallahassee, Florida, in the Sidney Foster piano studio, the age differences were reversed, for the teacher Foster was now thirty-two-years-old and the student seeking to study with him, Carlisle Floyd, was twenty-three-years-young and also a faculty member at Florida State University. His remembrance of Sidney is stated in his letter of July 7, 2007:

> I first met Sidney in the fall of 1949 when he joined the faculty of Florida State University where I had returned to rejoin the same faculty after a year's leave to get a master's degree. We quickly became friends. After a recital I played early in the fall of 1949, I asked Sidney for his reaction, and he re-

sponded by saying that nobody really wants to hear an objective opinion from a friend . . . Taken aback by such directness, . . . I managed to convince him that I really wanted to know . . . His response was not complimentary. Nonetheless, I took his evaluation seriously . . . and asked if I could have some lessons with him. He agreed . . . IF I would be willing to start over technically from the beginning; and thus I began the familiar standard Foster overhaul . . . Even with all the previous experience I had—a master's degree and an orchestral solo performance—I had privately faced the fact that I was in need of technical help . . . I willingly accepted his conditions . . .

Thus began the relentless but patient and uncompromising training . . . which eventually transformed my playing. Although I worked with Sidney only the better part of a semester, it was by far the most important time I ever spent with a mentor: he was that rare combination of a teacher in the best sense of the word, and, at the same time, an insightful and articulate coach . . . He expanded and illuminated my musical thinking in such a way that it really has provided the touchstone for all of my musical growth since.

These sentiments are from the younger student who was also a faculty member at Florida State University in 1949, the highly accomplished librettist/composer, Carlisle Floyd. That was certainly a winning team, Foster and Floyd.

Foster's most important concept is that "One uses the keys rather than plays on them." An honest admission for most of us is that much teaching and early training results in an approach wherein we translate the notes and values onto corresponding places on the keyboard. According to Foster, "This is a wrong and deadly approach. One must learn to *hear*, use the keys to translate the printed page into tonal concepts . . . A familiar trap most of us have fallen into is that we convert the symbol on the page to a place on the keyboard which is then held down for the indicated duration. Instead, the keys are those extensions to the hand which enable it to produce those sounds which are music conceived in the mind's ear."

Technically, Foster's approach is to realize that the arm weight is the fuel so to speak in piano playing, as gasoline is the energy that is needed to drive a car. His patience in teaching us to relax, to learn to un-flex or un-squeeze with our hands and arms, we learn to strike the key and immediately relax the tension that it took to do so. In learning that, we gain control and endurance in our playing.

The concept of arm weight as the fuel in piano playing is also true for some other instruments. When I accompanied one of his students in cello class, I heard Bernard Greenhouse speak about transferring the weight of the arm through the wrist to the fingers. In an article in *The International Musician* (September 1969), the brilliant bassist, Gary Karr, described the difference between weight power and muscle power in playing the double bass. Mr.

Karr advocated freeing the wrist of tension, as it directs the weight of the arm to the hand so that the fingers utilize the weight-strength of the arm, rather than the muscle-strength of the hand. This concept is the same for pianists. Our wrists act like "doorways" for the free flowing of arm-weight energy. We have to keep tension out of the wrists.

Learning to play *up on the attack* rather than *slap or hit the keys* will also determine the quality of the tone we produce. The speed of the attack also determines the softness or loudness of what we play. To play really soft, *pianissimo*, we take the weight away by using less arm weight.

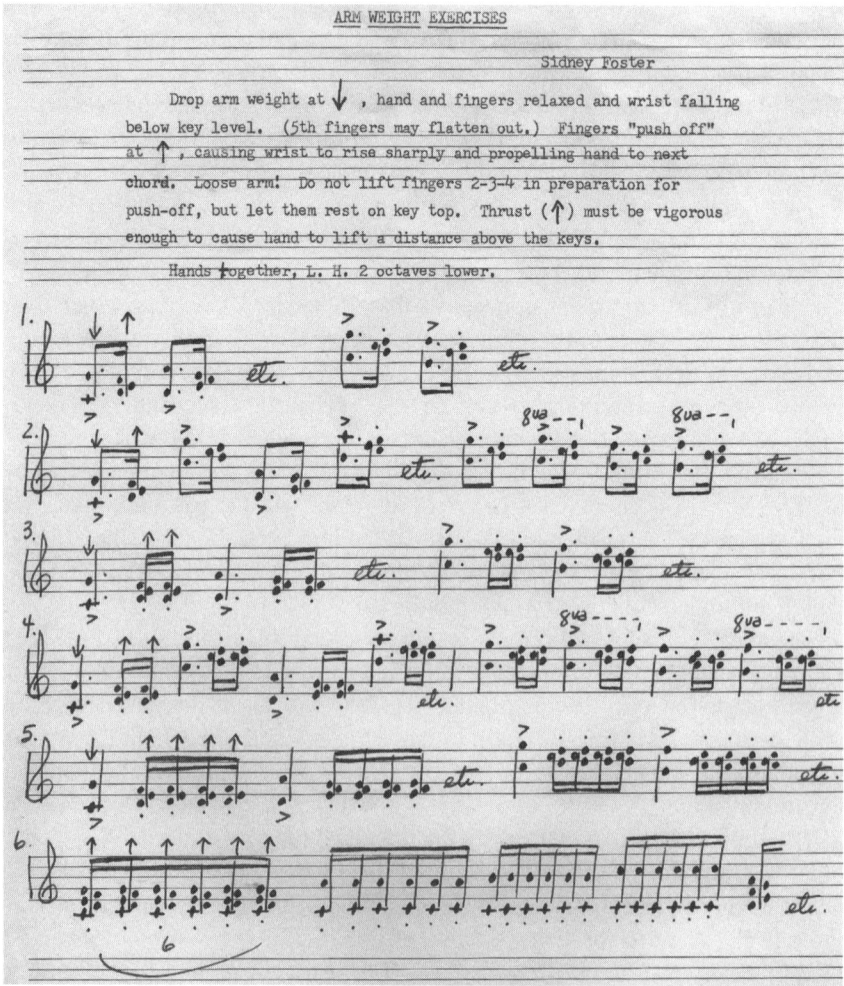

Figure 13.1. One of Sidney Foster's finger exercises. Copyright Bronja S. Foster, all rights reserved.

These are concepts that can be taught and learned with relative ease. Interpretation of style is also teachable. But the individual, innate talent that each of us has is the essence of what we will produce while incorporating a teacher's ideas.

Foster's tonal imagery and sense of expressive *rubato* were incomparable. A less-gifted pianist would try to imitate him. He would certainly observe and hear the extraordinary effects and coloring that he got with the unique use of all three pedals. Foster's wide feet allowed him to roll from the *sostenuto* pedal and on to the *una corda* without losing what he had been holding with the middle pedal, and all of this while using the damper pedal with the right foot. His pedaling concepts were creations dictated by what he conceived in his mind's ear—that was his unique talent.

His sense of realizing each student's unique qualities also tells of his teaching ability. He sensed what the student needed or lacked and imposed only that which would bring out the natural potential. When hearing several of his students play, one noted the common quality to all was a fabulous tone, power, and endurance. Yet they all sounded uniquely different.

In my own experience, when I came to his studio, I realized I was a shadow of what I had started with, when my previous piano teacher would tell me: "Be still. Stay close to the keys so that a sheet of typing paper cannot come between your fingers and the piano keys." I was stiff. Where I had previously enjoyed showing off, I now did not enjoy playing anymore. Foster's first words to me in that first private audition, after I played the first page of the Chopin *Ballade No. 1 in G minor, Op. 23*, were, "You have the quality in your playing that makes people sit up and listen; but you are very still, and your tone is rather small."

After explaining to him that I had not always been so still and stiff, he said to me, "Take the weekend off. Go to a movie. Come back on Monday, and we will start anew." And so we began. We had several mini-lessons for three weeks where he introduced me to how to play Hanon much differently than I had been told before.

Letting go of the keys in conjunction with the use of the damper pedal was most helpful in playing slow expressive passages in the Chopin *Nocturne in F major, Op.15, No. 1*, where before I had squeezed "with my wrist, arms, and fingers in an effort to bring out the *espressivo* of the Nocturne. It took me two years to incorporate his ideas—the physical approach—and to undo previous instruction. Most importantly, it had to be constant thinking to un-flex, not to squeeze the hands or arms. The analogy I used, even though I did not own an electric mixer, was telling myself to let my arm hang freely, to un-flex while I stirred furiously the mixture I was going to use to bake or cook.

In the third year of study with Sidney Foster, I started the Performance Doctorate degree. He commented after the first of my eight doctoral recitals—I had played the Chopin F minor Concerto—"Well, Imelda, you still have some problems, but you have made an impressive maiden voyage into the doctoral program."

Remembering his words, I kept trying, and some months later, after another recital performance, he took my arm, held it up, and said to whoever was standing there with us, "Look at that skinny arm! How does she get all of that power?!" The sparkle in his eyes and his comments made my day!

Collaborator—Indiana University

Performing for Sidney Foster included collaboration with other musicians. He thrived as a soloist, as a composer, and as a member of duos, trios, and larger ensembles. Some of his student assignments at the Curtis included playing for the cello lessons and public performances of classmate Leonard Rose. He once stated sardonically that "sometimes during Lenny's lessons, I received more of the music instruction from Professor Felix Salmond than did Leonard."

Foster's move to New York City, after his Curtis years, put him in touch with the young Isaac Stern. On many, many late nights, they would work on the duo literature which included Beethoven's Piano and Violin Sonatas. Their friendship was inevitable, even predictable, as both Stern's and Foster's fathers had emigrated from Kiev, and both Sidney's and Isaac's concert paths would often cross in the legendary Carnegie and Town Halls.

Without a doubt Foster's contact with various musicians like Salmond influenced his approach in matters of style, sound, and balance. As a teacher in chamber music lessons, he stressed the concept that the pianist in music ensembles has to play a strong bass as it, the bass in other words, is the bass for all the group, be it two, three, or more players. He also advocated the piano lid be opened all the way, as a closed lid mutes the piano sound and limits its coloring capacities. It is up to the pianist, however, to strike the right balance, raised lid and all.

Because he was a generous and direct individual, he often shared his past experiences with us, his students, to teach us not just music but public relations, diplomacy if you will. A case in point was one that occurred in the early years of his career when he lived in New York City. His management, National Concert and Artist Corporation, arranged an audition for him with the brilliant and famous violinist, Mischa Elman, who was well-established

Figure 14.1. Sidney Foster and his colleague, Josef Gingold, rehearsing Beethoven Sonatas. Photograph by Barney Cowherd. Courtesy: Indiana University Archives.

and looking for a pianist. Foster was given the address where Elman would hold the audition interview. After waiting for what was an inordinate length of time, Elman finally burst into the room where Foster waited. Foster recounted that initial encounter:

He was playing furiously and brilliantly, and when he finally stopped and acknowledged my presence, I said, 'Mr. Elman, that's a mighty fine sounding violin', to which he, Mr. Elman, quickly barked out, 'It's not the violin, you fool!' Needless to say, I didn't get that job.

In New York, and throughout his career, beginning with his Flute, Piano and Cello Trio formed in the early 1940's with the French flutist René LeRoy, and Hungarian cellist János Scholz, Sidney Foster played chamber music. At Indiana University, he collaborated with many colleagues in piano quartets and piano quintets with the Berkshire Quartet, the Beethoven Sonata cycle with violinist Josef Gingold, songs with soprano Agnes Davis, piano duets with Walter Robert, and many more performances with the wind and brass groups.

In addition to his Indiana University home based concerts, on one tour in 1962 that began in Europe and culminated in Japan, he was invited to play

Figure 14. 2. Violinist Toshiya Eto and Sidney Foster in Japan. Anonymous snapshot. Foster family collection.

a series of concerts with the violinist, Toshiya Eto, who had studied at the Curtis Institute and used the same management agency that Sidney used (Herbert Barrett Management, Inc.), scheduled in between solo piano recitals, concerto performances, and master classes in several Japanese cities. A grueling schedule he masterfully accomplished.

The range of his performances was as interesting as it was varied. Audiences in Bloomington and the surrounding Indiana area where Foster lived most of his life were fortunate to have heard him in chamber music, solo recitals, and as concerto soloist.

The Concert Pianist and the Old World Scholar
(*An Unusual Partnership*)

Sidney Foster played Johann Sebastian Bach beautifully. His interpretations of Bach's works—although not composed for the modern piano—that he and his students performed, nevertheless, were interpretative translations that kept as true to the spirit of the Baroque keyboard pieces as could be translated maintaining the expressivity that is inherent in Bach's ideas. Having said that, Foster used the modern piano's resources carefully—the pedals and their sustaining power—varying them through articulations and the concept of terraced dynamics to best project the composer's intentions.

A brilliant piano technique is required, obviously, to execute the extraordinary passage work and the contrapuntal lines in Baroque works such as those of Bach. Independence and interdependence have to be developed so that pedaling, with fingers holding down certain keys while letting others go in the same hand and/or in combination with both hands, has to be part of a pianist's physical repertoire of technical feats.

I recall one of those treasured moments of a concert that concluded by an unlikely choice of an encore that Foster played one evening in Carnegie Hall in 1965. He chose to play a Johann Sebastian Bach dance movement from the *English Suite in A minor*, which he ornamented elegantly and elaborately in good Baroque style. When he took his bow having finished the dance, two young boys, no more than eight- or nine-years-old, were not able to contain their delight of that interpretation, smiled broadly and clapped heartily. Foster smiled back at them, and in appreciation of their enthusiasm, he added a little wink to assure them he knew they were there on that front row in Carnegie Hall!

But when and where did Foster develop or learn Baroque style and practices when performing Johann Sebastian Bach's keyboard works on the modern piano?

In 1950 and 1952 the world-reknowned scholar, Willi Apel and Sidney Foster, the young concert pianist, were employed at the Indiana University School of Music in Bloomington. Dr. Apel, an old world scholar, had been an accomplished pianist with the additional credentials that included the published tome, *The Notation of Polyphonic Music* (1942), and the indispensable *Harvard Music Dictionary* (first edition published in 1944).

When Foster began teaching at Indiana University, his piano students were required to enroll in private lessons with him, and several of the graduate students also enrolled in Willi Apel's Keyboard Literature Course. From this curriculum they studied Johann Sebastian Bach and a gamut of the vast piano literature with Foster and the early Baroque pre-piano works with Dr. Apel. At a certain point, contradictions arose as Foster's piano students who performed Bach's works in Apel's class were told that their execution of the ornaments of the Bach works they were playing were "not adequate, perhaps spurious in interpretation." At their next piano lesson with Foster, they would play the Apel version of the ornaments in question. In this way and because of it, Foster became an Apel disciple in the execution of some ornaments in Baroque keyboard music, specifically those of Bach. The personal friendship Apel and Foster shared was fueled by their mutual respect for each other's professional integrity and accomplishment.

Architect of Piano Performance Doctorate

Renaming and rewording the well known Lola's Song from the musical *Damn Yankees* to "Whatever Wilfred C. Bain wants, Wilfred Bain gets" is an apt assessment of the recruiting pursuits of the deftly Dean Bain. His legacy was the monumentally prestigious music school at Indiana University that he developed over the course of his tenure as dean from July 1947 to July 1973.

What Bain wanted from the first time he heard Foster perform with the Dallas Symphony Orchestra was to hire Sidney Foster for his music school faculty (which in 1940 was North Texas State University and is now University of North Texas) in Denton. At that time, it was the best music school in Texas. However, in those early 1940's, the young concert pianist, Sidney Foster, was beginning to build his concert career. When Bain's offer came, Foster was gracious but declined it at that time.

In the interim, Dean Bain moved to Indiana University, where he continued his aspirations of developing a world class music school at that university, an artistic organization within an academic milieu. With his move, a handful of the North Texas faculty followed, and Bain's love of vocal music turned to an emphasis in opera. Be that as it may, his understanding was that the backbone of music schools is in great part the piano department, and Sidney Foster continued to be in his sights. In the meantime, Bain hired singers from the Metropolitan Opera for his faculty, and his new opera department blossomed.

Periodically Foster would get letters from Dr. Bain inviting him to join the Indiana University music faculty which Foster continued to politely reject. At one point, however, while Sidney was on tour, he received a phone call. "Dean Bain, how did you find me?" Bain answered, "I called your manager." This time Bain succeeded. After the tour ended in February 1952, Sidney Foster signed a contract to become a visiting artist at Indiana University, a position that would allow him to continue concertizing, which was also what Dean Bain wanted of his new faculty members.

At Indiana University, Foster had a class of undergraduate and graduate piano majors. He performed solo recitals, chamber music, and he became a piano duet partner with Walter Robert whom Dean Bain had brought from North Texas State University. Aside from their duet recitals, the two pianists became co-authors of the Piano Performance Doctorate Degree, one of the first in the top Schools of Music in the United States. With the input from scholars such as the renowned Willi Apel, whom Dr. Bain had engaged after Apel was denied tenure at Harvard University, the Indiana University piano doctorate was firmly established. It became and continues to be a formidable and rigorous degree with its requirements of ninety hours of course work. Although neither pianists/professors Foster nor Robert had earned doctorate degrees, their years of experience in the professional world made them aware that an artist must not only be able to play the piano artistically and competently, but the individual must be an articulate speaker as well as an artist who is a well-versed and capable writer.

The Classical/Baroque, Romantic, and Contemporary period piano seminars are challenging. The students have to prepare lectures and performances in a matter of days of the assigned monuments of the literature. With the seminar requirements in mind, the doctoral committee that hears prospective candidates for the doctoral degree assigns a piece to be prepared in forty-eight hours to gauge if that candidate has the capacity to learn quickly. In addition, the doctoral students present eight public recitals which are graded by the candidate's committee. A thesis-type of document is required; and students take both written and oral doctoral examinations.

At the time that this degree was proposed, the *Music Journal* published "THE CONCERT ARTIST AS COLLEGE TEACHER," an article by Sidney Foster for a Music Educators' Round Table Forum conducted in February 1956 by Indiana University's Jack M. Watson. Part of the article is quoted below:

> It has been said (was it by Bernard Shaw?) that "Those who can, do. Those who cannot, teach." The saying is just as contrary to the facts today as it has always been. Most successful performers have also taught, long before and since, let us say, Bach or Liszt. Today's performers are no exception, and both the famous and the not-so-famous are well identified as teachers. What *is* unique, perhaps, is the large number of fine performers to be found on college faculties. There is a simple reason for this.
>
> The growing recognition on the part of the colleges of their responsibility to the field of music has resulted in greatly expanded facilities for its instruction. The realization that in educating and equipping a musician they

are developing a first-class citizen and contributing significantly to the social welfare and culture of the nation is securing for music in the colleges no less an honored place than for medicine or law. In hiring Sidney Foster, Dean Bain engaged a first-class concert pianist who was an astute teacher. Foster had a passion for performing, and he developed one for teaching. His excellence was unquestionable, and like Dean Bain, he was a persuasive recruiter for the piano faculty. He successfully coaxed Abbey Simon, Jorge Bolet, and Menahem Pressler to join him at Indiana University, where those piano colleagues brought an artistic standard second to none.

Part Three

PERSONALS

John

Anna Diamond and Dorothy Foster DiFazio

Mana-Zucca (1891-1981)

Isabelle Vengerova (1877-1956)

Bronja (Miss Bronja Singer/Mrs. Sidney Foster)

From the *Grande* Scale to Gourmet Suppers

A Little Potpourri

John

Sometime in the early part of 1930 or 1931, the family of Louis and Anna, who now resided in New Orleans—all six of them, the father, the mother, and especially the children, Sidney, Edwin, Bill, and Dottie—were ecstatically awaiting a visitor. John is here! John, wonderful John!

The delight that children sometime exuded was justifiable because they were not easily fooled. They sensed and knew the genuineness of an individual. With John, they loved him well. It didn't matter, or perhaps they didn't notice, his contrasting chocolate skin to theirs.

John had known them in their first home in Florence, South Carolina. He had cared for them, cooked for them, consoled and cajoled them when it mattered. With Sid, when he was only three, with mother Anna and father Louis at work, John stacked books by the upright piano's keyboard so little Sid could get to the piano keys to play them. "Come on, Sid, let's have fun." And they did.

Years later, as an adult, Sidney Foster would see and evaluate people with regard to what they did and disregarded the extraneous. Thanks to this early friendship with John, Sidney Foster became 'colorblind.'

So it is with pride and gratitude that we acknowledge John for getting a music genius started and for shaping his attitude about goodness in individuals through example. After all, John was entrusted with the precious children by responsible parents. When Sidney himself became a father, it was easy to find a name for his first son, Lincoln. Whatever happened with John and his life, we hope was good because John certainly was.

Anna Diamond Foster and Dorothy Foster DiFazio

Anna Diamond, the lady that would become Sidney Foster's mother, was an only child. Her parents had come from Poland, and she was born in New York in 1888. In 1903, Anna's father died in a New York City hospital. She never studied music, but she enjoyed it and when she married Louis in 1914, she gave him an upright piano that went into their first home in Florence, South Carolina. Louis would play the piano as an amusement. Their children, however, would play it with a different outlook and outcome.

In both Florence and Miami, Anna was an important partner in her husband's varied businesses which dealt primarily with jewelry, as Louis was an expert diamond jeweler designer. Until her death in 1933, Grandmother Diamond lived with Anna's family. She was especially close to Father Louis and young Sidney.

Dorothy is the surviving sibling of Sidney Foster. She was the youngest of the four children Anna Diamond had with Louis. Dottie remembers mother Anna as a shrewd, staunch supporter of her children's 'musicianly' pursuits and as a "clearinghouse" for all that was relevant in their lives. Anna imposed her will on what instruments each of the four siblings would play. Unfortunately, this was hurtful and, indeed, damaging to her second son, Edwin, as his gift, like his older brother's, was in playing the piano; but mother Anna chose the cello for him. Eventually, Edwin would become estranged from all of his family.

Dorothy, the baby, began dance lessons when the family moved to Miami in 1926. In Miami, Anna would drive to the Coral Gables subdivision for Dottie's classes in dancing. Sidney became her earliest accompanist, and this duo would perform frequently for dance recitals.

At age four, Dorothy won a dance contest sponsored by a movie producer that got her a gold watch, a chocolate bunny, and some gold coins. But as a teenager, she began playing the viola. Her other artistic interests had been in sculpting and in photography, which brother Sid also enjoyed. However, the viola became the instrument she was most interested in and thus developed a professional career as an orchestral player.

She auditioned successfully for several orchestras which she played in including the New Orleans Philharmonic under Windingstad; the Indianapolis Symphony with Sevitsky; and with the New Orleans Philharmonic under Alexander Hilsberg, and in tours of South America. For many years, Dorothy played with the Radio City Music Hall Orchestra. She credits several professionals for teaching her the art of music making, viola playing, and the indispensable 'professional ropes,' with special note of Rafael Bronstein and Emmanuel Vardi of the NBC orchestra when Arturo Toscanini conducted it.

From their early duo childhood performances throughout their professional lives, Dottie and Sid remained close. When Dorothy married Louis DiFazio, an accomplished flutist who was also a Curtis *alumnus*, Sidney welcomed him heartily to the family as a third brother. Mother Anna's dedication in promoting her children's artistic efforts succeeded rather admirably.

Mana-Zucca (1891-1981)

Sometime shortly after the Foster family moved from Florence, South Carolina, to Miami, Florida, around 1925, the eight-year-old Sidney began performing in highly publicized music recitals. While attending the Conservatory of the University of Miami, he studied piano with Earl Chester Smith. After three years, according to a newspaper accounting, he was awarded a ten-year scholarship to any conservatory he chose to attend, which was to cover conservatory tuition, tutoring and living expenses.

Besides the University of Miami faculty and staff, Sidney attracted the attentive ears of Mana-Zucca Cassel (known formerly as Augusta Zuckerman), a brilliant performer and composer residing in Miami, who herself had been a soloist at age seven with the New York Philharmonic Orchestra with Walter Damrosch conducting her on a Beethoven Concerto. Mana-Zucca was so impressed with Sidney's playing that she offered helpful advice including her suggestion for him "not to cut his hair for a year while at the Curtis to hide his large ears." The reader will note on the photograph with young Sidney and Jacques Abram, following this page, indicating that Sidney accepted her advice.

Mana-Zucca outlived Sidney Foster by four years. Interestingly, she heard him play as a little boy and, decades later, as the mature, respected international artist he had become. In 1965, she gifted him with one of her published piano pieces, a piece called *Burlesque*, published by Congress Music Publishers of Miami, and she autographed it, "To the great pianist Sidney Foster, from his friend, Mana-Zucca. 1965."

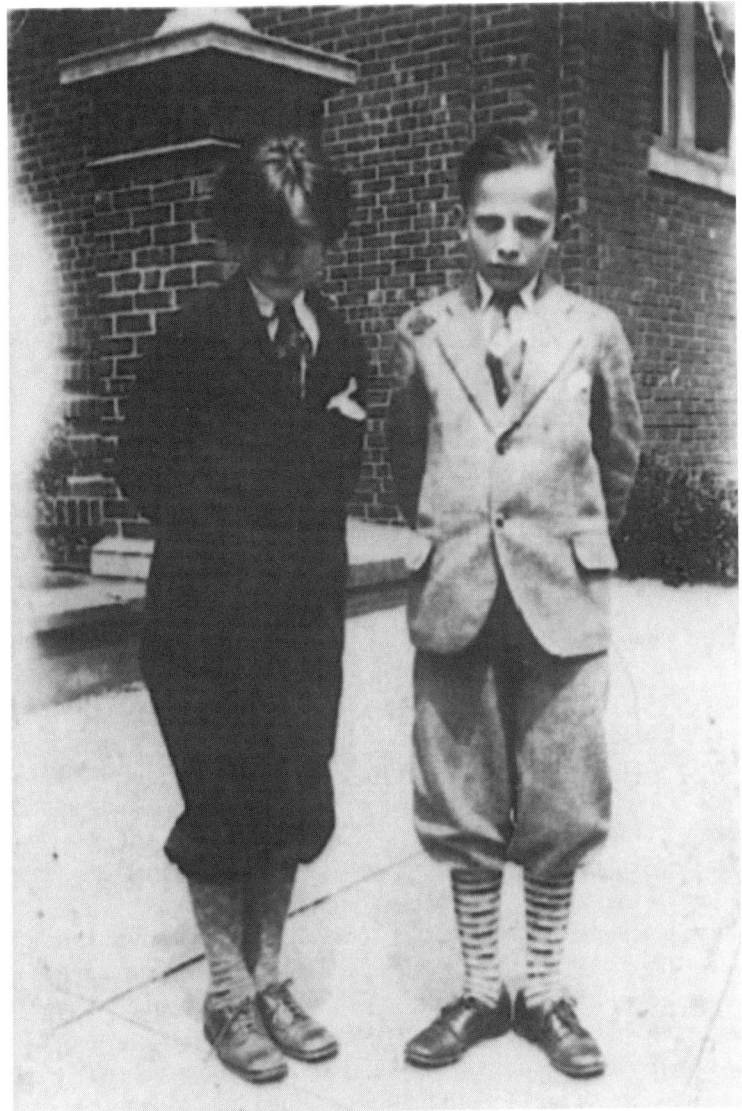

Figure 19.1. Sidney Foster and Jacques Abram as young boys. Sidney grew his hair long to cover his ears. Uncredited. Foster family collection.

Isabelle Vengerova (1877-1956)

One of the most lionized women piano pedagogues of the twentieth century is unquestionably Isabelle Vengerova. She came to the United States in 1921, after teaching for some time at the Saint Petersburg Conservatory. She taught in New York and at the Curtis Institute beginning in 1924. Her Curtis students included Leonard Bernstein, Samuel Barber, Gary Graffman, and Sidney Foster who were taught what she had absorbed from her major teachers—especially Anna Essipova, who was a Theodor Leschetizky protégé and Leschetizky's wife for a brief period of time.

Sidney's first encounter with Vengerova was as a ten-year-old, one of the handful of children who had been accepted at the Curtis Institute in 1927. He was then a confident young pianist and an extraordinary composer and improviser who had been acknowledged in Miami for his talents through several awards and prizes won in local piano competitions.

He was an attentive little child who took suggestions from established professionals quite seriously. When he walked into the Vengerova piano studio that autumn of 1927, he sported the long hair he had grown at Mana-Zucca's suggestion "to hide [his] big ears." If Vengerova ever commented about his hair, it is something we do not know. To her, this young ten-year-old would just be someone she could mold pianistically and musically as she did all of her students, young and old.

For two years, she imposed that Isabellelian will on little Sidney, sometimes scaring him and causing him to run out of her studio. The circumstances of his dismissal on this first attendance at the Curtis are clouded and somewhat secretive as records from the Institute were taken with the Executive Secretary when she retired. Vengerova may have been asked for a report about Sidney to strengthen the school's reason for ousting him. However, the rumors of mishandling of Sidney's financial backing from his hometown abound. And so it was that he was sent home in early 1930.

If Vengerova had been upset with little Sidney, she was even angrier with him on his re-acceptance at Curtis as a 'college-age enrollee' four years later—1934—because he was placed in the studio of David Saperton who assisted Josef Hofmann. Hofmann did occasionally hear Sidney play. After all, It was he, Hofmann, as the head of the Curtis, who had discovered this student years before.

Sidney Foster recounted to me the three different encounters with Isabelle Vengerova:

1. The infamous example as an eleven-year-old whom she frightened with her antics (refer to earlier piece in BEGINNINGS) over his shortcomings in a lesson on the Tchaikovsky *Barcarolle*;
2. her vocal displeasure when she learned that he had been assigned to another studio, not to hers; and
3. her calmer demeanor with him—the adult and accomplished professional who was now also teaching—as well as her lack of guile in not caring to conceal the realization that he, above all other of her former students, had understood most accurately her ideas and method of teaching technique.

He said this visit with her was pleasant and ended with a warm embrace when he thanked her for what she had done for him. Perhaps Mme. Vengerova had mellowed with the passing of time. She certainly was one of a handful of women who became significantly influential in Sidney Foster's life.

Bronja (Miss Bronja Singer/ Mrs. Sidney Foster)

In 1921, the Singer family emigrated to America from Przemyel, Poland. With great anticipation, all five of them—parents Rachella and Meyer Singer, sons Sina and Jacques, and five-year-old Bronja—settled in New Jersey. Unfortunately, father Singer died within a year of their arrival, and both the older sons Sina and Jacques took on the responsibility of keeping the family together.

Father Singer had been a cantor and an orchestral conductor in Poland. Jacques and Bronja would follow in his footsteps in their music pursuits— Jacques, a violinist, became an extraordinary orchestral conductor, and Bronja would develop pianistically. Although Sina had a flair for the theater and would produce theater shows yearly while attending college, he became a physician who practiced medicine until he died.

When Bronja enrolled in public schools, she was renamed 'Bessie' by the New Jersey school administrators because they told her, "The name Bronja does not exist here." Besides attending public schools, Bronja (Bessie) began piano lessons with an itinerant New York teacher, Victoria Danin, who would set up a studio in the Singer home. Years later Bessie and mother Singer moved to Philadelphia after Jacques enrolled in the Curtis Institute of Music. At age seventeen, Bronja would also be accepted at Curtis as a piano student.

In the Twenties, the immediate surroundings to the Curtis Institute contributed to the enhancement and artistic music development of the Institute. The Singer apartment was in that vicinity, and nearby was the home of the Stad family, who were musicians and collectors of rare musical instruments that they played. Eventually the Stads would establish the American Society of Ancient Instruments.

It was in the Singer home that on one afternoon in 1933 the sixteen-year-old Bronja came home from gym class to find Jacques and Maurice Stad,

Jacques' friend, engaged in friendly banter with another visitor from Boston who was seated at her piano showing off doing 'pedal tricks." Jacques and this person, Sidney, were emphatically discussing the merits of Oscar Wilde. Because Bronja looked up to her older brother Jacques as an authority on everything, this younger man came off as officious and arrogant! Propitiously, the following year, 1934, Bronja and Sidney became classmates as members of David Saperton's piano class. Others in their Curtis class included the composer/pianist Sol Kaplan, Mason Jones, the French horn player, Leonard Rose, the cellist, the soprano Virginia MacWatters and several other outstandingly-gifted music students.

In 1937, Rachella Singer died suddenly, just as Jacques was to embark on his first conducting post with the Dallas Symphony Orchestra, a job for which he had been recommended by Leopold Stokowski. After graduation from Curtis, Bronja joined Jacques in Dallas in late 1938. While she lived in Dallas, she played chamber music with some of the musicians from the Dallas Symphony Orchestra. However, in late spring 1939, Bronja moved to New York City, where she lived with her friends, the Oppenheimers, until momentously, on October 29, 1939, she married Sidney Foster. The young couple had earned their Diplomas from Curtis. They shared important values and dreams, and in late autumn of October 1939, they began their life together in Manhattan.

Other Curtis friends would also move to New York; they followed and helped each other, whenever needed. And with all of her devotion and might, Bronja encouraged her young husband to compete and to continue to develop repertoire for his career as a concert pianist. Just two months before their first wedding anniversary, Sidney learned the Brahms *B Flat Piano Concerto* which he would submit as the entry piece for the newly-established Leventritt Competition for Pianists that was held in September 1940. This triumphant event became one of many happy times they would share as a couple and later as a family.

From the *Grande* Scale to Gourmet Suppers

It takes physical energy to play the piano and food is unquestionably the necessary fuel. Sidney Foster's early years were spent in the southern United States: his birth place, Florence, South Carolina, Miami, Florida, where at age nine, he began his formal lessons on piano; and New Orleans, Louisiana, where he lived with his parents and three siblings between the two intervals when he was a scholarship student at the Curtis Institute in Philadelphia. The South undoubtedly influenced his gastronomical preferences. Just as the sound of music made him want to be a composer, his enjoyment of food drew him to experiment in the kitchen.

From 1934 to 1937, Sidney Foster lived in Philadelphia attending classes at Curtis, enrolling in the requirements for the Artist Diploma. In the fourth year, beginning in the summer of 1937, he moved to New York to live with his recently widowed mother and siblings, Dottie and Bill. He commuted by train weekly to Philadelphia to complete the remaining requirements for the diploma which included recital performances.

Beginning in June of 1937, the Curtis Institute awarded him a monthly financial assistance of $45.00 (forty-five dollars) until he graduated. His good friend and cellist classmate, Leonard Rose, also received financial aid, and this monthly allowance permitted both Leonard and Sidney to live in Manhattan and commute to Curtis every week.

Most of the time train commutes were uneventful for the Curtis fellows. However, on October 30, 1938, there was quite an uproar that rattled almost everyone. The broadcast of *The War of the Worlds* on the radio was presented as a series of news bulletins which many listeners misinterpreted as an actual Martian invasion in progress. There was pandemonium in the streets when the Curtis chums, Sid and Lenny, arrived on their train commute. That was an unforgettable Halloween treat!

In New York, the Foster residence on Seaman Avenue in Washington Heights had six residents: Mother Anna Foster, sister Dottie, brother Bill, and three Curtis music-a-teers—Sidney, Leonard, and Mini Knopow, a violist who would later marry Leonard Rose. This had to have been quite a household. So much music making and so many mouths to feed! According to Dottie, the sole survivor from these times, the three gentlemen slept in one bedroom; the three ladies slept in the only other bedroom. Sidney's piano was in the living room where, still in his pajamas, he would practice two hours daily. Lenny practiced cello in the bedroom; and the violin and viola got the kitchen and the bathroom. But practice sessions were short as the Curtis students were individually music whizzes! Household duties were distributed fairly, and peace under one roof was kept at bay among the personalities.

It was in this arrangement that gourmet chefs were born . . . Sidney and Leonard learned to cook dishes they had tasted elsewhere, while inventing new ones. Many years later, Sidney Foster's fascination and ability to prepare food continued to develop, and it became evident to us friends and students alike. Often there were events at Indiana University that called for gatherings in the Foster home in Bloomington. All of us—his piano students—became his music and food disciples. All four of the Fosters—Bronja, Sidney, and the two sons—were most hospitable. Their home was always a place we could go to in relaxed times or when life became difficult. We were their extended family.

Shortly after I arrived for piano graduate study at Indiana University, the Fosters invited all of us students, new and former ones, and a sprinkling of faculty members to an after-concert reception in their home. It was at that gathering that we were introduced to the artichoke. Unbeknown to us, the artichoke had a special history with Mr. Foster. However, much of the time, aside from that dinner, the marinated artichoke hearts would be just part of very tasty salads. Sometimes some white crumbly cheese topped this garden opener.

I tried all the 'gourmet' plates they served, abandoning my former habit of raking away any strange ingredients, a practice that annoyed my mother as she served her meals.

Most Sunday afternoons we would have piano class in the Indiana University recital hall where those of us who had pieces ready to try out would play, and the rest of us, 'the audience,' would critique our performances. It was a forum that encouraged performing and taught us to listen critically in order to voice intelligent, constructive criticism. And when those lovely Indiana autumn and spring Sundays permitted, our piano class would caravan in several cars to Brown County State Park for early picnic suppers of frankfurters, thick hamburgers unknown to commercial burger fast-food chains, and always healthy green salads with the ubiquitous artichoke!

One late afternoon, I stopped unannounced at the Foster abode to drop off some flowers. When I rang the doorbell, Mr. Foster greeted me with a somewhat quizzical expression, but asked me to come in. He apologized for not being able to ask me to stay for supper, "but this time I don't have enough of everything to serve you. You see, this evening I'm going to teach my sons how to eat whole artichokes, and Bron just bought for four. Next time, she'll buy an extra one." I told him not to worry, that my impromptu visit was just to bring them the bouquet, not to stay for dinner. He went on to explain that that supper had induced a bit of reminiscing for him about an experience from his teen years when, as a fifteen-year-old, he had arrived late at a formal dinner in New Orleans to play for a banquet. The dinner had started long before he arrived. After he finished playing for them, he was served dinner beginning with a strange new dish he had never seen before. By necessity and with some trepidation, he had had to ask the lady seated next to him what this was and "how do I eat it . . . ? "This green flower," she explained, "is an artichoke." So on this evening when I stopped by, Sidney Foster was serving 'Artichoke 101' to Lincoln and Justin, his teenage sons, taking them through all the steps of "buttered dipping, and scraping of leafs between clinched teeth, so they could successfully manage this awesome green flower, should the social opportunity arise!

Occasionally and unexpectedly, somewhat by accident, some of us students offered to help in the kitchen with dinner preparations. On one special dinner for an out of town guest—the mighty maestro Dimitri Mitropoulos—Dallas Weekley happened to run into Mrs. Foster at Bartlett's Food Store on Third Street while he shopped. She asked Dallas to help with dinner preparations, which he did. What a treat! Dallas met the *maestro* as a consequence of being part of a trio of chefs for that celebrated Mitropoulos evening.

Indianapolis was a mere fifty miles north of Bloomington, and, on rare occasions, there would be colleagues of Mr. Foster's who would perform with the Indianapolis Symphony Orchestra. He would inform us so that if our schedules permitted, we could go hear the concert. There was one evening when Alexander Uninsky was the soloist with the orchestra. The evening away from studies took on an air of celebration—a dinner in one of the big city's restaurants before the concert, and the excitement of meeting the artist, a friend of our teacher.

A wonderfully 'neat' place Mr. Foster introduced us to in 'Nap town' was Sam's Subway, known for its fabulous deli and dinner offerings. I think the deli menu reminded both Sidney and Bronja of their Curtis days because as I ordered a sandwich with corned beef, a 'Reuben,' they both gleefully told us that they ate this sandwich with Russian dressing almost daily in Philadelphia. So I tried the Russian dressing for the first time, and then I topped my order with a superb cheesecake, also a new taste for me, which they explained was a Sam's Subway specialty and one of the best they had eaten. That evening produced a continuance of Russian culture: Uninsky playing Prokofiev and my introduction to Russian dressing (with the added bonus of cheesecake).

Those of us 'Foster children' who dined often with our beloved surrogate parents would be treated to tasty tuna melts, spaghetti with mouth-watering sauces made from scratch, and unforgettably-unique sandwiches layered with mountains of meats and exotic cheeses. And once at a small gathering, Mr. Foster emerged from the kitchen with hands in mitts that held a platter. What was this? We had already eaten sumptuously through several courses. As the first Chef Sidney encountered, he asked, "Imelda, do you know what this is?" Negative. This final course became a ceremonious event—my introduction to Baked Alaska which I enjoyed and he relished preparing and serving.

Marinades were often spur-of-the-moment creations from items that he found in the kitchen cupboards. Those experiments flavored the salmon or swordfish he served often. One cocktail sauce he put together for the shrimp did necessitate passing out white facial tissues as there had been too liberal a portion of horseradish put into this creative concoction.

The facial tissue distribution was repeated at another get-together when, after one of my visits home to Texas, I brought back a gift for him of stuffed jalapeño peppers. The look on his face after he sampled the juice with the tip of his little finger is still an unforgettable picture of his panicked eyes as he commented, "Imelda! This is really hot!" Although Mrs. Foster and one or two other guests tried the jalapeños, the peppers were never to return to the Foster's dinner table. When I consider my humble Texas background, I look back in amazement at the variety of tastes I acquired when I chose Sidney Foster for a piano teacher!

I graduated with two advanced piano performance degrees from Indiana University and, throughout my years as a university student, there was a continuance of learning from the *grande scale* in his piano studio to the *gourmet delights* of the Sidney Foster kitchen.

A poignant postscript includes the life of his elder son, Lincoln. Years later, Lincoln left for graduate school to study chemistry with a renowned faculty at the University of California in San Diego. In California, he earned his living by house-sitting. Later, in his early entrepreneurial business ventures, he opened a charming, trendy gourmet restaurant that he named, Carnegie A440 Pizza Hall. Unforgettable those two—father and son.

SID'S ZUPE

Ingredients

1. A pound of lean beef or lamb (preferably the shank)
2. What you have of parsnip, parsley, celery, celery root, tomatoes, and a little piece of cabbage
3. A pinch of thyme, a bay leaf, six to ten peppercorns, salt to taste
4. A cup of raw barley
5. Water to the top of pot.

Preparation

Simmer slowly for four or more hours. Add fresh vegetables (or frozen) two to three hours before serving, if desired. Serve immediately. This delicious soup will serve approximately eight to ten persons.

A Little Potpourri

This section contains numerous anecdotes associated with Sidney Foster. While they may appear unrelated, they all remain, fixed forever, as wonderfully telling and heart-warming in the author's "mind's eye" of her beloved mentor.

TED TOWNE: AKA SIDNEY FOSTER

"Where can we hear the 'Fab Man About Town, Ted Towne?' Just go down to 1 Fifth Avenue in New York, to the club called *Number One, Fifth Avenue*. Then go back to summertime 1938!

You'll find him there! He can play anything that he knows and anything you can hum for him that he has never heard before; and, on rare breaks, he'll practice a little of the square stuff. You know, Chopin...His jazz arrangements of your requests will greatly entertain you.

Never mind the gal that waits for him at his table. She is just his sister, and they are both just kids. But Ted . . . well, he is some jazzer . . . *Numero Uno* on the great Fifth Avenue!"

IF YOU MUST DRIVE

"You got the job . . . Congratulations, Imelda! I'm thrilled for you, and I know your folks are happy too. Let me give you some good, yet unsolicited advice . . . , well, actually two pieces of advice:

1. Don't discuss your salary with anyone, especially 'friends.'
2. Don't tie up your first year's salary on a brand new car.

Once you start your work assignments there, you may not want to stay; or, they may not want you to stay. You don't want to 'get stuck' with making payments should you find yourself out of employment. If you must own a car, I can help you find a reliable and affordable used car. Oh! You don't know how to drive a car? Well, I can teach you how to drive a car. You're good with piano pedals, and driving is easier than playing the piano. But you have to be better at driving because you don't want to hurt anyone, including yourself.

Thank you, Mr. Foster, for finding 'Blue' for me. It is a wonderful 1954 Oldsmobile. And thanks for co-signing the bank loan with the Bloomington National Bank. I feel very lucky—free driving lessons with an expert, and 'Blue' even has air-conditioning. I wonder how that will strike the Vermonters?

"Lady, your car has air-conditioning? You won't need it here!" And that winter, and the next, and the next . . . the three years 'Blue' and I lived in Vermont, we didn't need it, never used it.

PS Back Pedal

When I got back to Bloomington that summer (1965) with 'Blue,' I almost ran into Mr. Alfonso Montecino, the Chilean pianist, who had just been hired to teach at Indiana University. He smiled when he recognized me and asked me how I liked his 'new-used' car. "Sidney found it for me!" We both drove off in our new-used Sidney cars!

PPS Luncheon, circa 1965

As lunch was being served to the couple and the waiter walked away, a distinguished gentleman approached the table and began offering an envelope to the gentleman who was dining. But as things became clearer, the diner exclaimed: "Oh no, Mr. Smith. Your dealership doesn't owe me a commission for the cars I've helped my friends find. I just did that as a favor to them!"

THE LAST BARK

The long sad faces at 405 Jordan Street were most unusual. So was the quiet house. Conversation was subdued. Viggie was gone. Viggie was short for Ludwig, the fifth member of the Foster household, a black and honey-brown Dachshund who had been struck dead by a car earlier that day.

Figure 23.1. Sidney and his beloved "Viggie," short for Ludwig. Photograph by Lincoln Foster. Foster family collection.

Everyone loved Viggie and Viggie loved everyone back. He used to get close to me because he loved the Estee Lauder "Youth Dew" perfume I wore. I think Viggie was Sid's dog, but we'll all miss him too, and Sid hid his broken heart admirably.

As I approached 405 Jordan Street later that week in summer 1960, I heard a light *staccato* bark. "Justin, what is his name?" "Well, we haven't decided on a name yet." "Not to worry; one will hit you as you walk down the stairs one of these day." As it came to pass, one summer day shortly after the new bark was heard, "Patty Foot, is that you? Here's a bone for you. Oh, you would rather have chocolate cake and cheese?" "Of course," was the expressive look on Patty Foot.

AMBER SKIES

"Do you know what that is, Imelda? The skies above . . . Have you seen those colors before?" "Not where I come from in South Texas do we see that kind of colored display in our skies." "Up here in the North in autumn, we get a glimpse of the Northern lights, the *aurora borealis*."

On my way to my first piano lesson with Sidney Foster, I saw this different sky for the first time. I was already madly in love with Indiana: those glorious autumn colors shimmering on the trees and now the translucent, ever-changing *aurora borealis* in the sky!

TIME TO LEAVE

I went to Mr. Foster's studio to bid my farewell. He said, "You've come a long way, Imelda. Keep doing things for yourself so you can continue doing things for others. Be creative . . . !"

Part Four

DEFINING PERFORMANCES

Memorial to His Father, Louis (1937)

Concerto Highlights (1954)

From Fliere to Foster: To Russia, with Love (The Russian Tour, 1964)

The Boston Premiére of Bartók's Third Piano Concerto (April 1965)

Memorial to His Father, Louis (1937)

During Sidney's second year at Curtis, in late 1935, his father Louis suffered a fatal heart attack. As the eldest son, just eighteen-years-old, Sidney accepted the responsibility of taking over whatever duties and obligations lay ahead with respect to his mother and three siblings.

He traveled to New Orleans and found a rooming house for his mother Anna and sister Dottie. He cleared their present home of what he determined to be unnecessary belongings and went back to Curtis taking his brother Bill, whom he helped enroll in public schools in Philadelphia, and entrusted his brother Edwin, to a respected friend, Frank Miller, a professional cellist in the Minneapolis Symphony Orchestra for lessons and for living arrangements.

Early the following school year, he returned to play for the memorial service for his father held at the Roosevelt Hotel. Most fittingly, he played the Chopin *Funeral March* and his piano professor Saperton's piece, *Zephyr*. Afterwards, Sidney took his mother and sister back with him to Philadelphia to live. But in his final year at Curtis, the three of them and brothers Bill and Edwin all moved to New York City into more comfortable living quarters. There Sidney would teach privately, and with the modest stipend from Curtis he could live with his family and commute by train to complete the remaining requirements for his Curtis Artist Diploma.

What each of us does at stressful times and consequent events defines us. Our actions say who we are. In playing for his father's memorial services, Sidney Foster honored the man who had brought him up. His assuming the role of head of his family eloquently defined him.

Concerto Highlights (1954)

Springtime signals new beginnings. For Sidney Foster, the spring of 1954 put him and a select group of thirteen musicians traveling by bus to fourteen concert dates performing piano concerto movements. That *Concerto Highlights* tour was the Sidney's brainstorm, who at age thirty-seven, decided to add 'conducting' to his artistic endeavors. Foster had already been a concerto soloist with numerous orchestras including his 1941 debut with the New York Philharmonic. He had played many solo recitals and also as many recitals with chamber music ensembles. He had composed, and he had taught, but he had never conducted an orchestra. On some of his dates as concerto soloist, he had wished that he could also conduct, for *tempo* alone can be a point of disagreement between soloist and conductor.

With this tour, wishing became a reality. The elite traveling group included a string quintet (the bass as the fifth member); oboist David Abosch, from the Colorado Symphony Orchestra; flutist Louis DiFazio, Sidney's brother-in-law. Clarinet, trumpet, French horn, trombone, bassoon, and percussion completed the congenial touring chamber ensemble.

Walter A. Gould, brother of Morton Gould, managed and arranged the dates, even joining the group on several of its concerts. Foster played the concertos, conducted them, and delivered short lectures on the music and their ensemble. He even did some of the reductions of the orchestral scores. The works that were performed were single movements of the Grieg *A minor Concerto for Piano and Orchestra* (first movement), the slow movement of the Chopin *E minor*, the first movement of the *B-flat minor Concerto* by Tchaikovsky, and all of the Gershwin *Rhapsody in Blue*.

The tour cities included New Bedford, Massachusetts, Ashtabula, Ohio, Manitowoc, Wisconsin, as well as cities in Illinois, Michigan, and Pennsylvania, Chattanooga, Tennessee, and the Texas cities of Dallas, Baytown,

Figure 25.1. The *Concerto Highlights* tour. David Abosch, photographer. Courtesy Imelda Delgado.

Corpus Christi, and Texarkana. After the Texarkana concert (probably their last one), Foster insisted that the bus take them all to his former home town of New Orleans, where the gourmet pianist treated his little orchestra to dinner at Antoine's Restaurant.

Musicians are no different from anyone else. They love good food, good company, and good conversation. Those musicians were treated better than usual. The oboist and the first violinist married and returned to Colorado, where they are still making beautiful music together. Sidney Foster's *Concerto Highlights* tour—his venture in conducting—was the happiest of collaborations. With Foster, *tempo* was not an issue. It was just music in motion.

From Fliere to Foster: To Russia, with Love (The Russian Tour, 1964)

Music and all arts manage to survive at crucial times when the political intrigues hold the entire world hostage. On those rare occasions, certain individuals find their way to the concert halls in the art Meccas . . . Manhattan, Milan, Moscow. In 1963, Yakov Fliere, the Russian concert pianist accompanied by his representative impresario, came to New York. He made his American debut playing the Rachmaninoff Third Piano Concerto with the New York Philharmonic with Leonard Bernstein conducting four concerts on October 10 through 13. As one of Russia's distinguished virtuosos who also taught, Fliere made the most of his visit to America by attending concert performances in New York's renowned venues.

It was thus that Mr. Fliere and the Russian impresario heard the pianist Sidney Foster in Carnegie Hall three evenings later on October 16, 1963. Foster's program included the obligatory standards: the Beethoven *Appassionata* Sonata and the Schumann *Kinderscenen, Op. 15,* which gave an easy basis for measuring and comparing him to other artists. Along with those works, Mr. Foster programmed the formidable, seldom-heard Rachmaninoff *B Flat minor Sonata* and the very American Dello Joio Third Sonata. Foster's opening piece—the intriguing Bartók *Dirge, Op. 8B*—immediately mesmerized his audience, and an audible hush lingered at its close. As one of America's "pianistic heroes" as Harold C. Schonberg intimated in the *New York Times,* October 17, 1963, Foster played most impressively, exhibiting his titanic technique and masterful interpretative powers. Mr. Fliere and the Russian *impresario* were so impressed that they initiated negotiations for an invitation to have Mr. Foster play in Russia during the 1964-65 season of concerts the following year. The Concert Bureau in Russia would arrange the tour—not our State Department.

When Mr. Foster returned to the Indiana University campus to resume his teaching, a great excitement arose among his students and colleagues about his upcoming Russian tour. After all, at that time, not too many artists from any countries played in Russia. The few that did, came by invitation only after a rigorous scrutiny of their credentials, both artistic and political.

Mr. Foster was very eager to perform in Russia, but his usual upbeat attitude was displaced with the reality and a skepticism that "some political situation will arise and events will be canceled. I won't hold my breath on the materializing of this tour."

The invitation to perform in Russia was extended to Foster in October 1963. A month later, on November 22, our beloved President, John F. Kennedy, was assassinated. Our world was suddenly and cruelly shattered. At Indiana University, in the music school corridors, students wept unabashedly and the faculty, for the most part, revealed a solemn demeanor. On the day of President Kennedy's funeral, Monday, November 25, Mr. Foster left a handwritten note on his studio door canceling lessons that day:

"It is such a depressing time. No lessons today."

Slowly time passed. Despite our glumness, we had to move on. At the Foster's traditional Thanksgiving dinner for those of us who could not travel to our far-away homes, Mr. Foster remarked that "this tragedy I feel can bring about qualities in the man who is now our President (Lyndon B. Johnson) that will make him a good and effective leader."

From time to time in the ensuing months, while all of us lost ourselves in our work, snippets of information about Mr. Foster's upcoming Russian concert tour would surface in conversations. Excitement began building again, and gradually the Russian tour became a likely reality.

Foster was asked to submit three or four different programs and several concerti. From them, the Russian Bureau would select what they would hear, or wanted to hear. Being the outstanding and responsible professional that he was, Mr. Foster kept up his full schedule of teaching (twenty-five hours weekly) and attended committee meetings. Additionally, his schedule included practicing that enormous amount of solo and concerti repertoire that the Russians had picked for the *twenty-two concerts to be played in thirty days in half a dozen Russian cities.*

Finally, both Sidney and Bronja Foster were off to Russia in early November 1964. Sidney played in the most prestigious concert halls: the Conservatory Great Hall in Moscow, the Tchaikovsky Great Hall, also in Moscow, the Leningrad Philharmonia Hall, and the Concert Hall in Minsk, where he performed with the Belarussian State Philharmonia.

The Russian audiences loved him! They went wild on the first concert in Moscow on November 12, giving him thunderous applause and coaxing seven (7!) encores from him after the final Prokofiev group, including the

Ninth Sonata, Eight of the *Vision Fugitives,* ending with the *Toccata.* After the last note, much of the audience crowded backstage to meet him and then accompanied him to his hotel—somewhat like baseball fans may react in America after a World Series game or as fans reacted to a Beatles concert.

The concert schedule was demanding: a Moscow concert on November 12, a second Moscow concert the following night, November 13, with a different program, Leningrad on the 14, 16, and 17; a Tiflis recital November 19 and a concerto in Tiflis on the 21. In Erevan, he played two recitals and a concerto; in Baku, another recital and a concerto on two nights, two concerts in Rostov-on-Don on December 2 and 4 and a final recital in December in Kishinev.

There were some interesting experiences the Fosters encountered during their month in Russia. Because Bronja had been born in Poland, documents, such as her birth certificate, had to be submitted as well as her passport to pass Russian government scrutiny. In a postcard that Bronja wrote to me, she mentioned arriving in Moscow after "many lovely and comfortable flights" two days before Sidney's first concert. The Russian government provided them with a guide, "a lovely blonde," who took Bronja shopping on their second day in Moscow. Their first evening in Moscow, they heard "an excellent pianist, Lazar Berman. Foster later told us that "we enjoyed his concert very much."

When they arrived at their hotel in Baku, a gentleman approached Mr. Foster who took him on a walk in a nearby park 'to talk.' The man basically asked Sidney Foster to take back some material (papers) to a relative in Chicago. The man claimed to be from an intellectual circle and stated, "We know how things really are; I hate to involve you in these matters . . . " at which time Sidney Foster interrupted the man's spiel and declared, "Please stop. I am a guest in your country, and I want to be a good guest. I cannot comply with what you are asking me to do with these documents."

This experience and the presence of another Russian gentleman in another town (perhaps Tiflis) whose hotel room was directly across the Fosters', whom they had seen before, back stage after a concert and who had most articulately and knowledgably commented on "the exquisite Mozart, and so forth," made both Mr. and Mrs. Foster wonder if they were being 'set up' for a possible contrived political incident with this gentleman and the man in the park. So, from that moment on, they started whispering to each other in their hotel room.

Aside from all of the extra-musical events, be they as they may, the Russian tour for Sidney Foster was a great triumphant success, one he was prepared for, and one he truly relished, despite, once again, the grueling schedule and demands on a prepared repertoire prepared by the Russians themselves. The Russian people wanted him to return, but just as life goes, some things never materialize as individuals move on.

It is most heartwarming and professionally reassuring when outstanding artists from different countries can earn a respect for each other because of the quality of their abilities and their generous spirits. Yakov Fliere was a distinguished Russian pianist, but more importantly, he was a selfless individual who wanted his compatriots to experience the artistry of the American he himself had first heard in New York. It was through his artistic influence that he was able to bring Sidney Foster to Russia.

In *Tass News*, the declaration after the Moscow performances stated, "Sidney Foster is one of the most impressive pianists to visit Moscow this century"

POST SCRIPT AT CARNEGIE HALL (1966)

It was my privilege and good fortune to have been a Sidney Foster piano student, and like many of his students at Indiana University who would finish a piano degree and go off to earn experience and a living, I would return for additional academic work in order to have the opportunity to study with him again. At the time of his Russian tour in late fall of 1964, I had left Indiana University to begin a post as a piano instructor at the University of Vermont in Burlington. This placed me geographically close to Montreal, where I traveled to hear Richter, and to New York City, where I went several times to hear my mentor in Carnegie Hall. In late 1966 a rare experience presented itself for me to visit Carnegie Hall on three occasions to hear the legendary Vladimir Horowitz on Sunday afternoon, November 27, Sidney Foster on Tuesday evening, December 13, which would be his last concert in Carnegie Hall; and on Wednesday December 14, Emil Gilels.

Horowitz played Scarlatti, Chopin, and Rachmaninoff. Before the concert, as I stood with hundreds of others in the standing room only area, the composer Aaron Copland strolled by, all alone, looking for his seat. Two weeks later, on December 13, I would hear Sidney Foster, and the following evening I heard Emil Gilels' concert. Attending those three concerts gave me a basis for comparing all three outstanding pianists in the same great venue.

Earlier, in the spring of 1966, Mr. Foster had judged a piano competition in Uruguay, and at that event, he heard a young and enormously-talented pianist, Alberto Reyes. Later that year, in the summer of 1966, Alberto enrolled at Indiana University to begin his study for a Bachelor's degree in Piano Performance with Mr. Foster. Characteristically, the Fosters took Alberto into their home to live when he first arrived in Bloomington. In late October of the same year, Mr. and Mrs. Foster, Justin, and Alberto came to New York City to meet friends and to see Mr. Foster's concert manager at the Herbert

Barrett agency. They spoke with me before leaving Bloomington, and I made plans to drive to New York City to see them and to hear Emil Gilels play in Carnegie Hall.

Our visit in their hotel room at the Salisbury Hotel, located across the street from Carnegie Hall, is unforgettable. I loved the Fosters—my second family—and reconnected with the young pianist Alberto from our days earlier that summer in Bloomington. While we were catching up on several music matters, Norman Dello Joio, the composer, called and dropped by for a visit. It was my first time meeting him. Three years later, I would be instrumental in inviting Mr. Dello Joio to be the guest composer at the Annual Contemporary Music Festival at Del Mar College in Corpus Christi, Texas, my home state and where I would move to after my teaching experience in Vermont.

Eventually the hotel visit ended as the Fosters had accepted a dinner engagement with Sol and Mrs. Kaplan. Alberto and I were given tickets to the Emil Gilels concert for that evening.

Gilels played two sets of Beethoven Variations: the *32 Variations in C minor* and the *Variations on a Russian Theme*, the Liszt B minor Sonata, and the *Waldstein Sonata* which showed off his fantastic double *glissandi* (I think Russians excel in double *glissandi*; Richter had also tossed those off in the *Alborada del gracioso* when I heard him earlier in Montreal).

After the concert we went back stage where Mr. Foster planned to introduce Alberto and me to Mr. Gilels. However, as the crowd gathered back stage, Mr. Gilels' representative came down and informed us that Mr. Gilels wasn't feeling well, but that "he would like to speak with Mrs. Foster." So Bronja Foster went to the Green Room where Mr. Gilels spoke briefly with her. When she came back, the back stage crowd was breaking up. We listened to what message she had from Gilels: "Sidney, Mr. Gilels wanted me to tell you, 'Thank you for the Rachmaninoff Sonata'." Gilels had heard Foster play it the previous night, also in Carnegie Hall.

Mr. Foster's playing of the Rachmaninoff *Sonata in B-flat minor* was the first I had ever heard of that work, and I heard him play it on several programs. I thought he played it wonderfully, but this statement coming from the famed Russian piano virtuoso, Emil Gilels, was certainly weightier than mine.

That occasion of Gilels' concert in Carnegie Hall two years after Sidney Foster played in Russia was a special post script to Foster's tour. Gilels' praise coupled with Yakov Fliere's conviction of Sidney Foster's piano artistry and his successful efforts to bring Foster to tour Russia would put these two high-powered Russian artists concurring that Sidney Foster, the American concert pianist, belonged to a unique league of performers, the one they belonged to as well.

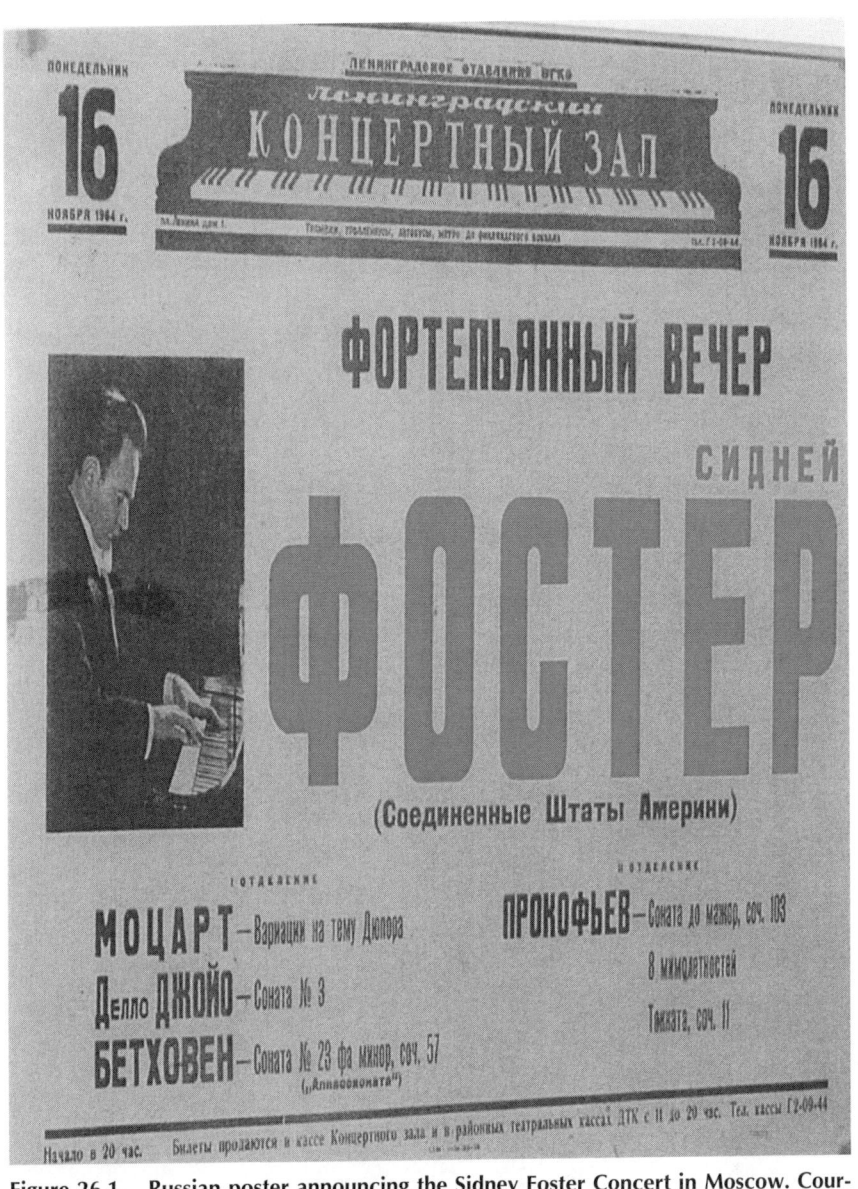

Figure 26.1. Russian poster announcing the Sidney Foster Concert in Moscow. Courtesy Imelda Delgado.

The Boston Premiére of Bartók's Third Piano Concerto (April, 1965)

After returning from his most successful and exciting Russian tour of 1964, Sidney Foster began learning and preparing the Bartók *Third Piano Concerto* for his engagement with the Boston Symphony Orchestra which had been by invitation from the conductor, Erich Leinsdorf. Foster had never played the Bartók Third, and Boston audiences had never heard Bartók's last work there,

Figure 27.1. Sidney Foster with Aaron Copland, April 1965. Previously unpublished photo taken by anonymous Baldwin publicity photographer. Foster family collection.

EIGHTY-FOURTH SEASON • NINETEEN HUNDRED SIXTY-FOUR–SIXTY-FIVE

Twenty-third Program

FRIDAY AFTERNOON, APRIL 9, at 2:00 o'clock

SATURDAY EVENING, APRIL 10, at 8:30 o'clock

AARON COPLAND, *Guest Conductor*

BUSONI..........................."Rondo Arlecchinesco," *Op.* 46
        (First performance at these concerts)

RUGGLES..........................."Portals," for String Orchestra
        (First performance at these concerts)

BARTÓK................Concerto for Piano and Orchestra, No. 3
    I. Allegretto
   II. Adagio religioso
  III. Allegro vivace
        (First performance at these concerts)

INTERMISSION

BRAHMS................Variations on a Theme of Haydn, *Op.* 56a

COPLAND............................"Music for a Great City"
    I. Skyline
   II. Night Thoughts
  III. Subway Jam
  IV. Toward the Bridge
        (First performance at these concerts)

SOLOIST
SIDNEY FOSTER
Mr. FOSTER plays the Baldwin Piano

BALDWIN PIANO   **RCA VICTOR RECORDS**

Figure 27.2.

although he had composed it in 1945. Originally, Bartók had conceived this music for two pianos to be played by his wife, Ditta, and he, both of whom played two piano concerts infrequently.

Foster learned the work quickly and with ease. However, for unknown reasons, Leinsdorf withdrew from his commitment to conduct the Bartók. Instead Aaron Copland was engaged for the concert that featured Copland's *Music for a Great City, Portals* by Ruggles, works by Busoni and Brahms, and the Boston première of the Bartók, with Foster and Copland collaborating.

The Symphony Hall was packed with audiences at both performances, the matinee on Friday, April 9, and the Saturday evening concert April 10, 1965. I was fortunate to have heard the fabulous Saturday evening performance and witnessed the standing ovation the orchestra gave Sidney Foster when the piece ended. Three Boston newspapers, the *Boston Globe*, the *Jewish Advocate*, and the *Sunday Herald,* covered the concert performances with favorable reviews of Foster's playing.

Part Five

Finale

1976: A Bicentennial and a Centennial

The Final Curtain

A Farewell Letter

February 7, 1977

1976: A Bicentennial and a Centennial

The last favor I asked of my mentor, Sidney Foster, was advice on how to go about getting an appointment at the Steinway & Sons Company to select and purchase a concert grand for the Recital Hall at the college where I taught, Del Mar College in Corpus Christi, Texas. It was May 1976, and the dean of my music department had given me the assignment to go to New York to make the selection, as the college had provided for it in its yearly budget. Knowing the demand for a nine-foot Steinway Concert Grand, I knew it would be easier to buy a pair of shoes than to buy a Steinway!

Sidney Foster was in New York City at the time. It was late May—the bicentennial year and, coincidentally, the Twenty-Ninth International Leventritt Piano Competition that was in progress. He was there as one of the judges which included the pianists Gary Graffman, Claude Frank, Leon Fleisher, Richard Goode, Nadia Reisenberg, Gitta Gradova, Rudolf Serkin, Mieczyslaw Horszowski, Rudolf Firkusny, William Masselos, and conductors William Steinberg and Max Rudolf. An interesting fact of Foster's being a judge at that time was that he had been the first winner in the first Leventritt of 1940, and now he was judging what would be the last Leventritt to be held.

When I spoke to him about buying the Steinway, and asked him how I might get an appointment with the Steinway & Sons Company, he sounded agitated, but nevertheless he told me: "Pay for a piano, and pay in advance." In essence, "Buy time with it until Steinway has several instruments that they can let you try out when they give you an appointment." So it was that advice that I followed. As our college had the appropriate sum that could be transferred quickly, I called the Steinway & Sons Company. I selected a beautiful instrument with the help of my ears and those of another Foster student who lived in New York City with her husband, a first chair string bassist with the New York Philharmonic. I had also asked a respected piano technician from the New York area that had been recommended to me for his advice. That Steinway D arrived in Texas a few weeks after my trip to the Steinway & Sons Company, New York. With minor adjustments and tuning, that concert grand began its residence in the Wolfe Recital Hall at Del Mar College, where I was teaching and where it is still the favored instrument used by the current piano faculty members and by visiting pianists and touring artists.

In our conversation that May day in 1976, which would be the last time I heard my mentor's voice, we talked about the possibility of my playing solo recitals in several European cities. Additionally, during our phone conversation, he disclosed his opinion that Alan Ball should have made the second round in this Leventritt.

In 1940, after Edgar M. Leventritt's death, there were just a handful of those events worldwide. Now, there are over 300 piano competitions! Considering the plethora of such events currently in existence, the Leventritt Foundation was now using its resources in different, equally constructive artistic merits and endeavors. Thus, that 1976 Leventritt was the last Leventritt Competition. And as in the three previous competitions, no First Prize winner was selected.

Sidney Foster had come full circle with the Leventritt Competition—opening it up as its first winner and closing it in his participation as one of its judges. Later, cash awards would be given by the Leventritt Foundation, but not as a result of winning a competition.

The following month, on July 26, 1976, would mark the centennial of Ernest Schelling's birth in Belvidere, New Jersey. Schelling's widow, eager to promote celebratory tributes, gave Sidney Foster the score to the *Suite Fantastique, op 7*. On three occasions, just months before he died, Foster performed that superb suite for piano and orchestra to enthusiastic audiences.

As I think about the lives of Sidney Foster and Ernest Schelling, I find that there exists a "circular set of circumstances." Although they were separated by decades, there were curiously auspicious omens. In 1938, when Foster won the MacDowell Award, Ernest Schelling was the President of the MacDowell Association and would continue to be so for eleven years until his death on December 8, 1939.

Schelling also played his last solo piano concert in Town Hall on January 3, 1939, just weeks before Sidney Foster played his February 10 debut recital, his prize for winning the MacDowell Competition. What is the likelihood that these two pianists met and/or heard each other's 1939 Town Hall performances? At twenty one-years-of-age, Sidney Foster, if he did meet and hear Schelling at that time could not see into the future. But in 1976, perhaps he remembered and would realize the remarkableness of that time long gone. Now he paid homage to Schelling, another American pianist like himself, who had been a child prodigy and one who had also composed.

The Final Curtain

For a career that began so brilliantly and because he was truly not a 'run-of the mill' pianist, the name Sidney Foster did not become a household word as it should have. He had a spectacular technique, a unique expressive interpretative ability, phenomenal power and a thorough knowledge of style for all of the considerable literature he performed.

His repertoire was vast, encompassing works from the Baroque to the 'traditional' contemporary school of composition which excluded works that exemplified the serial technique and those of chance (aleatoric). If one heard him play the same work twice or more—be it a Beethoven, Chopin, or Prokofiev Sonata, or any other work—each performance would be stylistically correct, but the interpretation of the works' musical events would be different and fresh with each performance as that particular interpretation developed further, according to how he had started the piece.

Sidney Foster was a handsome man with dark hair, skin of alabaster quality, and finely chiseled features. His clear brown eyes would direct a steady gaze that projected the appropriate meaning of the moment. His uncanny ability to express and articulate his thoughts and ideas was extraordinary. But several significant attitudes came into the big picture:

- He was modest, never one to promote himself. He believed in himself and his ability, but he was not driven by blind ambition.
- His sense of ethics and his temperament conflicted with the need for an aggressive business sense that was imperative in the relationship with a management that would advocate for more concert dates for him.
- Competition was especially ferocious for pianists; and at certain periods in the business world of the arts, the perception of "those in the know has been that management and critics alike glorified and promoted the import

above the domestic," be it the French or Russian artists. In those days, there was a demand for the very young . . . , of course gifted, but especially very young.
- Illnesses—his and those of his family's (his younger son, Justin, was stricken with poliomyelitis at two)—brought about interruptions and necessitated changes of direction affecting his concert career. As a dedicated family man, being there for his family took precedence over his career. But Sidney Foster was born to perform. Concerts were timely venues for the music his hands could deliver. His original desire had been to compose so he did not obsess for full concert seasons which dwindled with the passing of time. However, both his management and former students from far and wide secured significant engagements each season.

The early concert dates with the New York Philharmonic are accomplishments that can never be discounted or taken away. The 1964 Russian tour of twenty-two concerts within one month that included orchestral and solo recitals was truly spectacular for him as it would have been for any performer of his caliber.

An important and revealing exchange that transpired between a colleague and him, before he went on the Russian tour, is an accurate index of Sidney Foster. His colleague advised him to call for a press conference when he arrived in Russia, but that was not his style. He had never been driven by self promotion, so he did not heed his friend's advice. Nevertheless, the Russian tour of 1964 was a smashing and defining time in his career.

Furthermore, at a time when recording had become *de rigueur,* Foster did not record for major labels. However, there were the Musical Heritage Society recordings of two Mozart Concerti with the Vienna Chamber Orchestra— where Sidney composed his own Cadenza for the C major Concerto— and the Clementi *Sonatinas,* which, in his interpretations, elevated those works from simple pedagogic pieces to expressive concert jewels. But recording contracts with RCA or Angel Records never materialized.

In chronicling the ebb and flow of Foster's career, it is imperative to address the reasons for the interruptions as they are directly related to his health. When he started on his own, it was fashionable to smoke; so he smoked to the point undoubtedly that it contributed and exacerbated his genetic predisposition for a cardiac attack. His father, Louis, had suffered a singular fatal one at age forty-four.

After a concert in Racine, Wisconsin, in November of 1955, Sidney was stricken with a most debilitating heart attack which necessitated the cancelation of his forthcoming Carnegie Hall recital that following week. He recovered from this serious illness, causing him to alter his life style significantly:

no more smoking, healthier eating habits, and the consumption of massive doses of vitamin C.

His teaching duties were resumed the following spring semester of 1956, and when he played his comeback recital in Carnegie Hall on November 23, 1959, the *New York Times* declared,

> The pianist's hair has some gray in it now. His playing too has matured. Mr. Foster played with the sort of insights that come when a man understands a work as a whole as well as its individual parts. It is fine to have him back!

Then in the summer of 1965, as both the Fosters drove to Indianapolis to pick up Angela, Joseph Battista's wife, on her return trip from a memorial service in Colorado for her husband, the pianist, they had a car accident. He suffered a broken leg. At least three Indiana music students with the same, not-so-common blood type, provided blood for the much needed transfusions. Again he recovered, never minding (too much) the telltale limp.

More unfortunately, as time was running out for him, the duties of his teaching post drained his energy with endless committee meetings, student recital hearings, and countless other obligations besides the more than twenty-five hours of his studio teaching load. When one enters the milieu of academe, some of those duties are not completely evident in the life of the faculty member.

In spite of all that, Foster never lost his sense of concern for others—his family, his colleagues, his students, and even strangers in need he encountered.

Some of us have had difficulty accepting his untimely death at age fifty-nine in that winter—February 7, 1977—because it was accidental and caused by hospital staff error. At the New England Medical Center in Boston, he had had surgery to remove an enlarged spleen caused by a complicated blood condition where his bone marrow gradually became scarred. The medical terminology is frightfully long—eleven syllables contained in three words beginning and ending with the letter *A*:

A G N O G E N I C M Y E L O I D M E T A P L A S I A

A slight, though important digression is that Bronja Foster, his widow, has a theory that this scarring of the bone marrow was caused by a drug since taken off the market, administered to him after his heart attack in 1955 to prevent the blood from clotting.

But, returning to his surgery in the Boston Hospital, it has been carefully documented that Sidney Foster had not eaten solid food for a significant amount of time prior to surgery. He was quite weak. The day before he died, the hospital staff brought him his food and medication, a pill, which in his weakened condition caused him to choke.

During a piano lesson many years ago, as I struggled to project my ideas in a new piece, sensing my frustration, he said sympathetically:

Imelda, life is about solving problems. It is like a series of curtains which we are compelled to open. When we succeed in opening that curtain, we see that there is yet another curtain and many, many more. So we continue pushing them back through our lives until the final one.

For this beloved mentor, the final curtain in Boston was not to be pushed back. On Tuesday, February 8, 1977, the *New York Times* obituary article carried the news: "Sidney Foster is Dead; Concert Pianist, 59, Won First Leventritt Award."

TUESDAY EVENING, FEBRUARY 8, 1977

After his death in the wee hours of February 7, 1977, in that Boston hospital, his family—Bronja and two sons—were surprised by the unexpected visit of the dean of the Indiana University School of Music, Dr. Charles H. Webb. He had flown to Boston to visit Sidney Foster and the family. The Foster family instead told him that Sidney had died. Dr. Webb, a pianist, was not Mr. Foster's student, although he had worked with him the semester his teacher, Walter Robert, was on sabbatical leave. But that dean was, and is, a man of great heart. As Lincoln Foster related to me, "Charles Webb helped us pack all our belongings from our hotel rooms and got us to the airport."

On Tuesday, February 8, I was on a plane to Bloomington, a trip to see the family and the first trip to Indiana when I would not see my mentor. That evening the gathering at 1224 Maxwell Lane was somber and sedate. Many of his piano students were there, some whom I had met and knew, all heavy-hearted trying to accept an absence in this familiar house that was distinctly strange.

At the fireplace stood a tall and exquisite arrangement of white bird of paradise, not the usual color for that flower. I commented about its serene beauty, and someone told me that it had been sent by Van Cliburn. As I looked around at those who had gathered in the Foster home, my eye caught the face of Mr. Baldwin, one of my doctoral committee members who was a close and dear friend of Mr. Foster. We acknowledged each other from afar, and I saw him dab at his eyes as inconspicuously as he could.

Suddenly, Helena, the Brazilian student, brought me back into focus with, "Imelda, you should have heard Mr. Foster's Schelling!" Schelling? Who and what was the Schelling?

The following morning, on Wednesday, I returned to Texas. I had a handful of recitals to play, but the name Helena had mentioned at the wake kept turning over and over in my mind as I went robotically through the motions of teaching and practicing. What a mentor! He was still teaching me. As the weeks went by, Schelling became a significant presence. The sadness eventually subsided and a comfort enveloped me as I began eagerly to work on the last lesson with my mentor.

A Farewell Letter

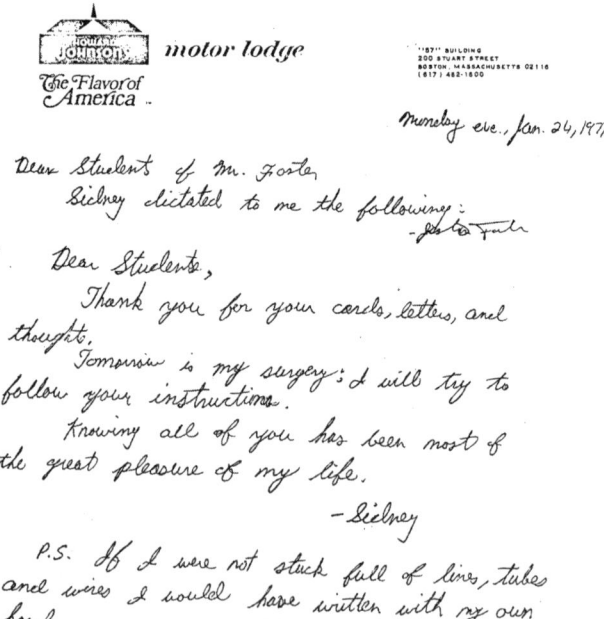

Figure 30.1. Copyright Bronja S. Foster, all rights reserved.

February 7, 1977

My mentor died on Monday, February 7, 1977, at 4:00 a.m. A curious coincidence was that it was also on an early Monday morning two years prior when my father died at 2:30 .a.m. I think it was 7:00 a.m. when the call came from Boston from a friend who was with the family, my mentor's widow, his two sons, and, more than likely Alberto Reyes, who was one of my mentor's brightest piano students. "Did you hear, Imelda? Our beloved teacher is gone."

On the day before (February 6), I had played a solo recital. When I arrived home that night, I felt a compulsion to turn on all the lights in every room of my apartment. As I look back thirty years, I believe that my sixth sense, my bond to him, was making me prepare a tribute, a message sent from one who loved and respected what he represented in my life . . . a true mentor.

A sense, perhaps a premonition, of what would transpire that Monday was my awakening suddenly at 6 a.m., which would have been 4:00 a.m. Boston time, and precisely the hour he died. So when Veda's call came, I knew, and a heaviness enveloped me.

That sorrowful Monday morning, as my teaching workday began, the first sounds I heard my first student play were the notes of Hanon, *Exercise No. 1*. Those C major five-note patterns cut into my heart. The first notes I had played at my first lesson with him were those very same notes.

I got through the next hours without crying. Around lunch time, Mary Bludworth, an adult student of mine, invited me to her home after her lesson, fed me lunch, and comforted me. She knew, and she was the friend that I needed at that hour. What we talked about or said is something I cannot recall. I don't even remember if she asked me to play on her Steinway piano, but I remember playing *Sadness*, an *American Prelude* by Alberto Ginastera. As I played, I hoped my mentor was listening to me because I infused it with my soul and with the lessons of music-making he had passed on to me.

Mary served a Paul Masson sherry which was in a brown heart-shaped glass container which she gave me to keep. For a long time, I kept that carafe, but with intervening events and with all that happens in the passing decades of our lives, I have misplaced and probably lost it forever, that heart-shaped decanter. What is not possible, fortunately, is to lose what my mentor gave me. That is comfort.

APPENDICES

Appendix A: In His Own Words: A Piano Workshop

Appendix B: The Students Speak

Appendix C: *Cadenza* to the Beethoven *Piano Concerto No. 3 in C Minor, OP. 37,* 1941

Appendix A

In His Own Words: A Piano Workshop

Some Important Principles about Piano-Playing and Music-Making

**SIDNEY FOSTER
DISTINGUISHED PROFESSOR OF PIANO,
INDIANA UNIVERSITY**

1. Develop the concept that one *uses the keys* rather than *plays on them*.

    This is a critically important idea. Much teaching and early training results in an approach wherein one translates the notes and values onto corresponding places on the keyboard. This is a wrong and deadly approach. One must learn to "hear"—that is, to use the keys in order to translate the printed page into tonal concepts. Hence, the trap into which many, if not most, have fallen is that of converting the symbol on the page to a place on the keyboard which is then held down for the indicated duration. Instead, the keys are those "extensions" to the hand which enable it to produce those sounds which are music conceived in the *mind's ear*, as it were.

2. Recognize the importance of the following principles of using the keys.

    a. The intensity (loudness or softness) of sounds results from the momentum with which the hammers strike the string. The faster the hammer travels, the louder the sound. This travel of the hammer is in direct relation to the speed of the descent of the key. It may be put, therefore, that the speed with which the key descends is what determines the quantity of sound—nothing else.

    b. The most efficient way to send the key down, and the most controlled, is to join the fingertip to the key as a fulcrum, thus engaging the leverage system of the arm to that of the piano. This is a way in which tensions are at a minimum—where one can say that the arm is allowed to swing most freely, loosely, hanging, and weighty, where wished.

c. After the string is struck, so long as the damper remains up, nothing can alter the sound. This is a fact which the wishful-thinker doesn't like. (There may be valid psychological reasons which justify pressing on the key after the sound is made, but it is important to understand that this does not change the sound in any way.)

d. *Legato*: A perfect *legato* comes from connecting the sounds. This means connecting the dampers—keeping the damper of one note up until the next sound is made. This can be done by keeping the key depressed, of course, as the key is connected to the damper in such a way as to raise it whenever it, the key, goes down. But it is important to recognize that the foot can do the same, via the pedal, usually more easily. This makes legato octaves possible, for example. Hence, connecting the keys is not important.

e. *Staccato*: *Staccato* means detached, but the important consideration is that it is the sounds which are detached. Of course, one detaches the keys in order to have the resulting *staccato*. (But, it is important to remember that one may also detach the keys and by means of the pedal produce the finest *legato*.) More on this later.

3. The basic "touches." By this is meant the ways to make sounds with the key.

   a. The pushing up by the fingers of the wrist and hanging arm for "running" notes, unaccented, between falls of the arm and wrist, which later produce accents. That is to say that the effort is by the finger--either in pushing the weight of the arm away from the key (therefore pushing the key down)—or in receiving the falling arm. But the important element is the relaxation of the arm and the activity, at the key, of the finger. Must be demonstrated.

   b. At the key, 'thrusting' the arm in the air by a sudden effort involving a strong contraction of the finger (or by one finger). Must be demonstrated. An important modification of this is the quick but gentle 'thrust' by which one plays 'syllabic' melodies. This relates to 2.d. above, which speaks about *legato*.

   c. The free fall of the arm onto a finger, or fingers, from a suspended position.

   d. A 'bouncing' touch (actually the combination of b. and c. just preceding) where on a chord or series of chords there is a falling which ends in a thrust on each chord (or single notes) so that as each sound is produced the arm is bounced into position to fall to produce each following sound. Must be demonstrated.

   e. A *staccato* touch, which results from a light (held up) arm so that the fingers can thrust each key down with sufficient speed (energy) without following the descent very far. Put another way, this means imparting by a shallow but quick effort enough momentum that the key will continue to descend although the distance the finger travels is slight, thus enabling the return up of the key at the earliest possible moment and the consequent drop of the damper, stopping the sound.

SUMMARY OF TOUCHES

The best way to play is that which leaves one in the best position to play the next note.

Tone

A good tone depends on a few simple factors. First, there must be a relatively large sounding melody line. This 'stage' or 'declamatory' tone differs from what I characterize as 'conversational' tone. It is a common failure to neglect the melody line, which should be projected with far more volume than the other parts of the musical texture. The amount of this melody sound is seemingly exaggerated to the uninitiated, and one must become accustomed to it.

Tone quality is related to subtle changes in balance of what is vertical, and to the subtle rhythmic and dynamic variations of the horizontal. Actually, all one can do on the piano is send the hammer toward the string slower or faster in order to produce softer or louder sound, but *quality* differences occur when certain overtones are more or less prominent. The prerequisite for making these quality changes is a keen and experienced ear—which comes from sensitive listening—enabling the performer to emphasize certain of the notes relative to others.

Pedal

The pedal is the "great emancipator" of the pianist. With it his hands are free. He does not have to hold down keys after their function (to cause the hammer to hit the string) is affected. The invention of the pedal made possible the great sonorities which distinguish *piano music* from early music. Paderewski called the pedal the "soul of the piano."

The purpose of the pedal is to keep up, as long as desirable, the dampers. This not only frees the hands from this mechanical activity, but enables the pianist to connect octaves, chords, great leaps, etc., which no other instrumentalist can do. Sonority and *legato* thus are made uniquely possible.

Appendix A

The student should learn to use the pedal as early as possible. It comes up where his instinct is to beat his foot. This is the first step in understanding its use. He should also know that the great, powerful 'harp' inside the piano case has dampers attached to the pedal so that he can learn the attitude that one 'opens up the harp'—that is to say, puts down the pedal, thus lifting the dampers, letting them down from time to time as the *ear dictates*, much as the harpist from time to time dampens the strings with her palms.

INTERPRETATION

Some random thoughts:

Musical notation is inadequate and unscientific and one must 'read between the lines.' This 'unwriteable' element constitutes the domain of the 'Interpreter.'

However, there are various small formal elements, which comprise the large entity of the entire movement, imbuing each with the character and 'content' as he perceived them. The form derives from rhythm, and the French analysis of pulse is a good basis on which to begin. It is shown in Figure A.1.

This allows the divisions, or groupings, shown in Figure A.2.

Examples:

I. Beethoven, Op. 10, No.3, First Movement.
Brahms, *Ballade, Op. 10, No. 1*

Figure A.1. The French analysis of pulse.

I.

II.

III.

and, in: $\frac{3}{4}$

and

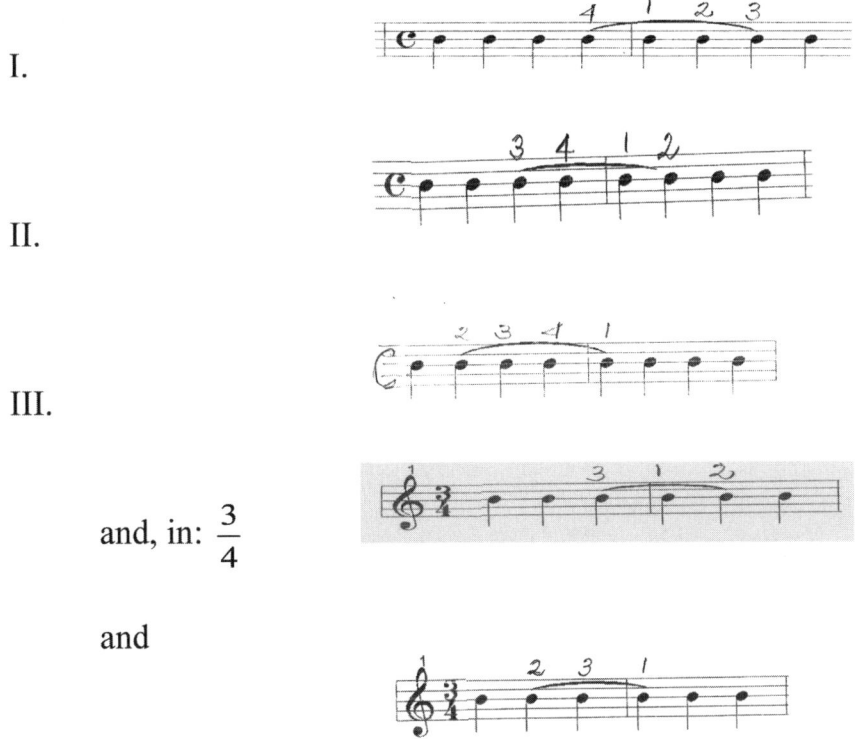

Figure A.2.

II. Schumann Fantasy, *Legend*
Beethoven, Op. 14, First Movement, second theme
III. Beethoven, *Rondo, C major, Op. 51, No. 1*
Beethoven *Sonata, Op. 110*, Fugue
Franck *Prélude, Chorale et Fugue*—second theme of *Prélude*
Mozart D minor Piano Concerto
(This is not to say that there is no music without up-beat. There is, but such is relatively rare. A good example is Mozart's A minor Sonata. The antithesis is the Prelude of Bach's A minor English Suite where every note is upbeat to the first beat note.)

Counting out loud is an important tool for the young musician. He or she should hear the up-beat quality spoken about above. However, it is terribly important for him or her to *establish* the beats rather than *identify* them. This means a good staccato enunciation of beats which the music follows, and not a 'sing-song' accompaniment which might follow the distortions one is trying to avoid.

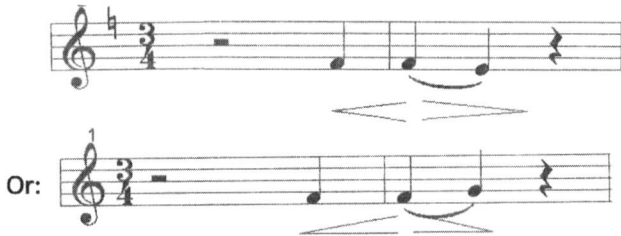

Figure A.3.

An important element, very expressive, which pervades all music from the earliest times to the present times, is shown in Figure A.3.

Phrasing: The slurs on the page, sometimes by the composer, sometimes by the editor, do not generally constitute phrasing. Phrasing must be understood in relation to form. A phrase is a small unit of musical form, and it is best grasped if one knows the so-called 'eight-bar period.'

A clear example of this form is the first eight bars of the first of the Schumann *Kinderscenen,* shown in Figure A.4.

As one sees—or, better, hears!—it is composed of four phrases. These are delineated by dynamics (and, perhaps, in the hands of the sensitive artist, a delicate *rubato*) and are not separated by a breath, by time, or other such primitive devices. These devices are really unmusical. One gives the phrase shape with loud and soft the same way an artist makes a circle into an orange with light and shade. In the phrase below, the triangle represents a dynamic stress, corresponding to the highlight in the orange alluded to above, toward which the melody is impelled and from which it recedes. A *crescendo* and a *diminuendo* are usually employed, as in Figure A.5.

Figure A.4. The first eight bars of the first of the Schumann *Kinderscenen.*

Figure A.5. A *crescendo* and a *diminuendo* are usually employed.

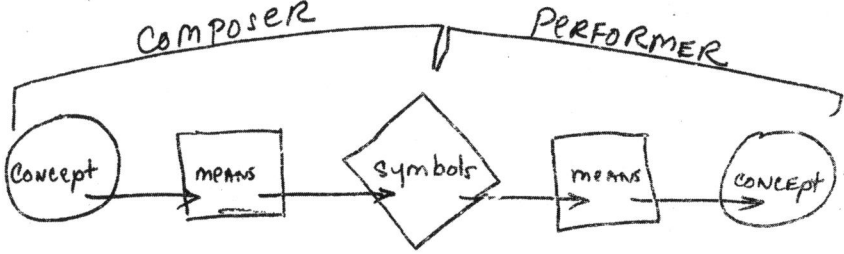

Figure A.6. Path of a concept, diagram hand-written by Sidney Foster. Copyright Bronja S. Foster, all rights reserved.

Appendix B

The Students Speak

Jane Abbott-Kirk—BM; MM in Performance, Indiana University; Professor of Piano, Baylor University, Texas; Clinician

Hans Boepple—BM; MM in Performance, Indiana University; Concert pianist; Professor of Piano, Santa Clara University, San Clara, California

Patricia Brady—DMA, Indiana University; Rachmaninoff Scholar; Professor of Music, James Madison University, Harrisonburg, Virginia

Lew Brandes—MM in Performance, Indiana University; Accompanist, Butler University, Indianapolis

Harry Coleman—DM, Performance, Indiana University; Private piano teacher, Pittsburgh, Pennsylvania; professional photographer; Recording engineer

Imelda Delgado—MM, DM in Performance, Indiana University; Professor of Piano, Del Mar College; Boston Records, Protone Records; Clinician

David Effron—MM in Performance and Conducting, Indiana University; Opera conductor, Eastman and Indiana University

Carlisle Floyd—Foremost librettist and opera composer; University of Houston, M.D. Anderson Professor

J.B. Floyd—DM in Performance, Indiana University; Concert pianist, Composer, Professor of Piano, University of Florida in Miami

Helena Freire—Concert pianist, recording artist and Professor of Piano, School of Music of the Federal University of Minas Gerais, Belo Horizonte, Brazil

Miriam Gargarian—BM, MM, DM, Indiana University; Private piano studio in Boston

Herbert Golub—DM Ed., Indiana University; Professor of Music, Kean University, New Jersey

Figure B.1. Imelda Delgado with Sidney Foster. Courtesy Imelda Delgado.

Robert Hamilton—BM, MM in Performance, Indiana University; Concert pianist; Professor of Piano, Arizona State University

Alan Hersh—DM in Performance, Indiana University; Professor of Piano, University of Kentucky, Lexington

Edward Kaizer—DM, Indiana University; Concert pianist; Jazz improviser; Professor of Music, Peoria College, Illinois

Chiu-Ling Lin—DM, Indiana University; Concert Pianist; Professor of Piano, Drake University, Des Moines, Iowa

Thomas Mastroianni—DM, Indiana University; Professor Emeritus, Former Dean, Catholic University; President, American Liszt Society

Caryl Matthews—BM, MM in Performance, Indiana University; WBAA, Purdue University, West Lafayette, Indiana

Joseph Matthews—DM, Indiana University; Professor and Director of Keyboard Studies, Chapman University, California, Duo Piano Concerts with Karen Knecht

Richard Morris—BM, MM in Performance, Indiana University; Clinician; Professor Emeritus, Cincinnati Conservatory of Music

Val Goff Norton—MM, Tulsa University; Doctoral candidate in Performance, Indiana University; Private piano and voice teacher in New York City; Chamber Music Performer

Welby Pugin—MM, Doctoral Candidate Indiana University; Owner and Business Manager, Ghent Montessori School, Norfolk VA; Arranger and accompanist for Virginia Children's Chorus

John Reitz—BM, MM, Indiana University; piano faculty, Kenyon College

Alberto Reyes—BM, MM, Indiana University; Concert Pianist, Winner of the Leventritt Prize and of the Tchaikovsky and Van Cliburn Competitions

Patsy Hodges Seybert—BM in Performance, Indiana University

Robert C. Smith—DM in Performance, Indiana University; Professor of Music, Vincennes University; Professional Accompanist

Eva M. Vouklizas—MM in Performance, Indiana University; Professor of Piano, University of Pennsylvania

Charles H. Webb—DM in Performance, Indiana University; Dean Emeritus, Jacobs School of Music

Dallas and Nancy Weekley—MM, DME, Indiana University; Schubert Scholars, Concert Duettists; Professors of Music, University of Wisconsin at La Crosse

Paul Wirth—MM, DM, Indiana University; Artistic Director of Central Minnesota Music School

Veda Zuponcic—BM, MM, Indiana University; Concert pianist; Guest Professor, Moscow (Russia) State Conservatory; Professor of Music, Rowan University, New Jersey

JANE ABBOTT-KIRK

Under The Influence: Seven and a Half Years to Life

I was first smitten by the sparkling eyes and expressive voice of Sidney Foster. It was the end of my sophomore year in high school, and Mr. Foster was in Corpus Christi for a performance with the symphony. My childhood piano teacher and family friend, J.B. Floyd, had just completed his doctorate with Foster at Indiana University. At J.B.'s request, I was given the opportunity to audition for Mr. Foster. This momentous meeting paved the way for two life-changing summers for this young high school student. Following my sophomore and junior years, I was privileged to study with Mr. Foster in the Collegiate Credit Music Course at Indiana University. These two summers and continuing lessons with J.B. provided a solid preparation for admittance to the piano performance degree at Indiana.

I had four incredible years of undergraduate study and a year and a half of graduate work under this inspiring and world-class pianist. Foster was and continues to be a major influence on my career as a performer, teacher, and person. The integrity and uniqueness of his teaching approach is legendary. All of us who were fortunate enough to study with him were in awe of his knowledge and musicianship.

The absolute highlight of every week was my lesson with Mr. Foster. Following close behind, were our afternoon Sunday piano classes in the Recital Hall. The lessons, piano classes, and Foster's compelling performances taught me the basic principles of sound, technique, phrasing, architecture, and repertoire.

The Big Principles

A thread common to Mr. Foster's teaching and playing is related to BIG. It was about developing a big tone with minimum effort, whether it was a rich, warm, wonderfully-projected melodic tone or a sonorous, round, chordal celebration. Quality of tone was always the defining criterion.

It was about finding maximum freedom in and from the arms to create power, presence, and control—allowing gravity and freedom of the arms to work in perfect partnership.

It was about the long line whose journey and timing compelled the listener to follow, arrive, and connect to the next line. Each line was created through thoughtful, fresh, craftsmanship and design.

It was about the overall architecture of the piece or movement and how the various sections related to and explained each other and created the overall big picture. The inevitability—one phrase to another and one section to another—was the overriding concern.

It was about the big giants of the piano literature and the growth and maturity that resulted from wrestling with the demands of this repertoire. This growth and maturity fed directly into smaller-scale works.

Random Reflections

What a privilege during coffee breaks to listen to stimulating and sometimes hilarious exchanges between Sidney Foster, Abbey Simon, and Jorge Bolet. They were like brothers in their obvious affection for one another. The teasing was unrelenting. This was a wonderful model of collegiality and friendship.

What an inspiration Mr. Foster's eloquent mastery of the art of verbalizing complex thoughts and artistic ideas was. He could always find the perfect wording and the most logical ordering of thoughts. In my own early teaching,

I tried unsuccessfully to imitate his style. In the end we all need to find our own way.

What a treat it was waiting for that encore moment on every recital when Mr. Foster performed his signature piece, Perpetual Motion by Weber. It was always so effortless and whimsical. All of us who had studied this piece were reminded of how delightful it could sound.

What a model of "paying forward." When I returned to campus (post degree) for recital preparations, Foster steadfastly refused any payment—a model I have made my own.

What a sign of the times, the 1960s, it wouldn't happen today. The Dean at the University of Kansas called Dean Bain at Indiana University, who in turn, called Mr. Foster, who in turn, called me to fill, sight unseen, a just vacated faculty position at Kansas University. What incredible trust and faith in Mr. Foster was demonstrated in this moment. And, what incredible naïveté for a 21-year-old, who hadn't even completed the MM recital, to accept such a responsibility. Mr. Foster's recommendation was the impetus for this bold new direction in my life. I am forever grateful.

HANS BOEPPLE

First Meeting Sidney

When I arrived in Bloomington in 1967 to begin my Freshman year at Indiana University, I had never heard of Sidney Foster. The only lead I had for a piano teacher was the recommendation of a cellist, who suggested I contact György Sebők, the collaborator of the great János Starker. When I went to Mr. Sebők's door and asked if I could be his student, he told me his studio was full, but to come back in the spring semester and see if there might be room then. The conversation took all of thirty seconds.

I did know one person on the Indiana University music faculty, Harry Farbman, who was both a violin professor and a wonderful conductor with whom I performed two concertos with two different orchestras in past years. I had lunch with Harry and his wife, Edith, and they immediately suggested I approach Sidney Foster; they knew of Sidney's teaching not only because they were faculty colleagues, but because their daughter, Patty, was taking lessons with him.

I knocked on Sidney's door, he answered graciously, inviting me in, and told me, "Hans, I have 28 students at the moment, and if I can possibly resist you, I will!" We talked, I played the first movement of the Barber Piano Concerto (that I happened to be working on at the time), and, finally, he said, "Well, I can't resist you!" And that moment represented one of the important and fortunate turning points of my life.

Sidney's Musicianship

In my very first semester, I was working on the Rachmaninoff Rhapsody with Sidney, preparing a performance with an orchestra in Southern California. In the eighth variation, there are some thick chordal passages, and Sidney used a similar section from one of the concertos to illustrate the similarity of their structures. He began playing the dense, 8-notes-per-chord area from the concerto, and then said, "But this isn't the right key." So he played it again, a few steps down, and said, "This isn't the right key either," went back up a step and tried again. Then he said, "Well, this still isn't right, but I'll just stay here," and he played this complicated passage with complete command.

The man could have levitated off the bench as far as I was concerned, and I would not have been more impressed. It took me half a year to absorb what I had seen and heard him do in that half a minute. He had an aural mastery and a relationship with the keyboard that I had not known before, or even thought possible. I immediately began doing transposition exercises on my own!

An Example of Sidney's Teaching

Sidney was working with another student on the Brahms D minor Concerto; I was there because I was playing the orchestral reduction. There is a complicated passage, and Sidney was trying to make a point to the student about how to shape it. But the student had another idea and wouldn't bend, so Sidney let it drop.

The next day at the next lesson, Sidney had written out by hand on manuscript paper, a short, simple three voice cadence using a suspension, which could have been written by Mozart. Sidney asked the student which of the melody notes he would emphasize, and the student pointed to the obvious note. Sidney then showed him that what he had written out was a reduction of the very passage they had discussed the previous day, and suggested that the Brahms passage should be shaped similarly. The student agreed.

It was an example of how Sidney never imposed his will as "the teacher." His teaching was often Socratic like this, his ideas springing directly from the score, and he preferred that students know exactly why they are doing what they were doing.

Sidney as an Artist/Teacher

Before I went to Indiana University, my notion of piano teaching was based on my impressions of the piano teachers I had known while growing up. My own teacher in Los Angeles had been an active pianist as a young man, but did almost no performing during the many years I studied with him. He only taught piano lessons, seemingly from dawn until night, and since he was my main model of a teacher, and since I wanted to be a pianist, I assumed the two activities were antithetical, and was therefore, certain that I didn't want to be a piano teacher.

That notion changed when I met Sidney. Here was a musician for whom no dichotomy seemed to exist; he was an active performer as well as a wonderful and devoted teacher; he blended the two worlds together perfectly. With this new image in my mind, and the idea that one might just be able to "have it all," I began to think altogether differently about the prospect of teaching.

About Dealing with Performance Anxiety

Right before my very first solo recital at Indiana University, I was warming up in Sidney's studio, when he came in and asked if everything was alright. I told him, No, that I was scared out of my mind, and that I knew I would not be able to play my best. I told him that it was a long-standing pattern with me, that I was resigned to playing maybe 75% of my best, and was pretty upset about it because I felt that I was well prepared.

Sidney, standing at the door, said something very simple, "Have you ever considered, Hans, that the recital is not about you? That it is about the music? People are there to listen to the music. Don't worry about yourself; be a musician out there and devote yourself to projecting the music as best you can."

That statement not only turned my whole head around, as well as the recital (which went very well), but has become the way with which I have dealt with nerve issues (and those of my students) ever since.

Sidney's Generosity

One weekend, my wife and I were going to be traveling to Chicago (the reason, I can't remember). When I told Sidney, he took out his wallet and gave me $50. I tried to refuse, saying that I was sure we wouldn't need it. But he said, "Well, if you don't need it, then give it back to me on Monday. But, if you do need it, you'll be glad you have it."

Sidney was the first adult in my life with a no-strings-attached generosity, and this was true in ways that had nothing to do with music.

PATRICIA BRADY

Confessions of an Eavesdropper

My memory fails me as to the specific time and date (1971 or 1972), but the deed is clearly and permanently imprinted on my brain. It was my first semester in the School of Music at Indiana University, arriving as a rather naïve graduate student from Memphis, Tennessee. Feeling lucky indeed to have been accepted into the esteemed Mr. Sidney Foster's studio, I was determined to do my very best to live up to that honor (and not diminish the efforts of my immediate past teacher, who was himself a former student of Mr. Foster). I diligently practiced and poured over every marking and comment that Mr. Foster made in my music, and looked forward to each lesson for more comments and things to fix.

But as the weeks wore on, it seemed there was little I could do to earn the positive feedback I so desperately desired. In fact, instead of giving more directions, Mr. Foster began to give fewer suggestions, and my lessons were shorter now. It seemed I would play, wait for the directions, receive a few shrugs and then be dismissed! Mustering up some courage after several frustrating sessions, I asked when he would give me more instruction as to what to fix, what to make better.

I think I will never forget his God-like thunderous response. It was a life-changing moment as he answered: "When you come in with some music ideas of your own!" and added, "You are not a blackboard for me to write on . . . Now go away and come back when you have something to say." Gulp . . . Talk about complete and utter devastation! I was so used to being the good student, following every instruction to the smallest detail, and now I was to come with MY OWN ideas! Pretty scary thought . . .

Well, tenaciousness is one of those qualities most Southern belles possess, and fortunately I was blessed with an abundance of the stuff (some also call it stubbornness). I began to analyze and study my music, listen to every recording of every piece, discuss heady issues of musicality with my classmates, and—here is the confession, kept a secret until now:

It was still warm that fall—must have been late September or early October, and the big window in Mr. Foster's studio was often open while he was teaching. I so admired some of the more experienced and successful students playing in our studio—and so desperate I was to learn what they were learning—that for several afternoons (quite a few, in fact), I secretly sat under the big fir tree outside Mr. Foster's studio—eavesdropping. Close enough to hear the playing and comments Mr. Foster made, taking in the discussions about phrasing, pedaling, voicing and other musical matters. When I heard engaging discussions about musical ideas and alternative ways to interpret a piece, I realized that I had been working so hard at following my teacher's directions, I had no direction of my own—a revelation. So I began a new tack. I had to be brave enough to jump in with both feet and swim. Not easy, but I couldn't bear to have such a great musician and teacher think I was a mindless wimp. It didn't happen all at once, but I began to take more chances and try out (what I thought were) dangerous exaggerations. Slowly, I became aware of a change in Mr. Foster's demeanor in lessons. Instead of scowling and disapproving glances, he began to have that wonderful twinkle in his eyes and a hint of a smile. I don't know to this day whether he was smiling at the fact that his clever manipulation was working, or that he admired my tenacity and willingness to try my darnedness. I'd like to think it was some of both.

As the weather grew colder and the window was closed more often, my covert activity was curtailed. I don't think anyone ever knew ("My God, I wonder if HE ever spotted me, sitting under his window, appearing to be studying, but taking in every word, every comment, and every gesture. If he did, he never let on, probably knowing how completely mortified I would be if he found out about my eavesdropping.).

Months grew into incredibly wonderful years with Mr. Foster (and with Mrs. Foster—whom I credit with insisting, against all my resistance, that I try broccoli—which I have fully grown to enjoy!) I learned so much about making music, and life in general during those years. No one could surpass the wonderful role model he was as a musician and as a person. Underneath the sometimes stern and gruff exterior was an incredibly warm and caring person. His expectations made you reach higher than you ever thought possible. To hear him play was absolutely awe-inspiring. His confident demeanor, complete technical mastery and ease, depth of musical expression, elegance, sensitivity and polish were unparalleled, providing the greatest lessons for us all. And the experience of knowing both Sidney and Bronja is something very dear that I have carried with me for all the years since that time. So many of the lessons we have all learned have spread far and wide to our own students, and even to their students—both lessons about music, and lessons about life. I often relate to my own students how two wonderful people so influenced my own teaching and playing.

So, there you have it. Guilty, but not the least bit remorseful. In my case, the crime paid off. How fortunate to have known the Fosters. They will always be a part of who I am and who my students are. And—I cannot possibly thank them enough . . .

LEW MCSWAIN BRANDES

The very first time I met Sidney and Bronja was during the summer of 1952. I had come to Indiana University for a summer of study with Sidney, prior to giving my senior recital at Florida State University.

Sidney and Bronja had invited me to dinner at their university apartment. Sidney had prepared a Chinese dinner for us and insisted on using chopsticks—(to my chagrin). Lincoln and Justin were adorable young boys (who called their parents by their first names!). It was a memorable experience, but certainly an unforgettable introduction to two people who would be extremely instrumental in shaping my life in the years which would follow.

I came back to Indiana as a graduate assistant and began work on a master's degree in piano with Sidney. I was a young, extremely shy, very sheltered, southern girl who had come up "North" to Indiana.

I experienced my first snow that winter of 1954 as well as the wonder of all the seasons on the Indiana University campus. Bronja and Sidney became my 'Foster Parents.' They opened their hearts and home to me. They enabled me, just by being who they were, to shed my southern prejudices, and to look at life and people in a new and different way—in a positive way! They were wonderful in every way.

As I look back on piano lessons with Sidney, I realized that he had the single greatest impact on my life (other than my own father) of any other human being on this earth. That was true then, at age twenty, and it remains true at almost 75.

Sidney not only taught me how to bring the piano to life, but about life, and how to live it—about truth, honesty, humility, fairness, compassion and goodness—and not by teaching it, *per se*, but by being the personification of all of these things. There were so many facets of his greatness as a performer, musician, teacher, conversationalist, intellectual—the list could continue forever!

He gave us all (his students)—(those who would succumb to Hanon and Czerny) the tools with which to create beautiful sounds with the piano. As a teacher, he was quick to get at the bottom of a problem and immediately find its remedy, be it technical or musical—but Sidney was just as quick to compliment when your own musical idea happened to work.

In that way, he showed his unusual capacity to give of himself unselfishly. He was not a jealous person. He recognized each of his students' talent, but more importantly, he enabled each to develop that ability to its utmost degree—so that the finished product was uniquely your own (and not a carbon copy of someone else).

What Sidney did (in effect) was to gift his students with the ways and means and insight to communicate the art of music. He taught us to listen, and adjust accordingly as you perform. He enabled us to see and hear the music clearly; to interpret; and then to project that interpretation beautifully.

Once, many years after I had graduated, I went to hear Sidney in a solo recital at the University of Illinois at Champagne. I remember he played a Beethoven Sonata. I sat enthralled at his performance! I told Bronja later that it was as if I had gone on a journey with Sidney, winding our way through a Beethoven Sonata—lingering here and there to discover a new inner voice (seldom heard), exploring new ways to execute a phrase—uniquely Sidney, but uniquely beautiful and thrilling as well as impeccable technically. He was a master performer!

He enjoyed performing and that was evident to all who were privileged to hear him. Bronja labeled him a musician's musician, and he truly was that.

On another occasion, I was present as he taught a master class to university students. He took a pencil and played the melody to Schumann's (of Foreign Lands and People)—along with its regular accompaniment. He played it beautifully (of course) while demonstrating the relationship of a melody to its accompaniment.

These are just a few of my reflections of those "good old days" at Indiana. I am almost 75 and I have never outgrown my love and respect for this giant of a man and his beautiful wife Bronja!

HARRY COLEMAN

Schelling: 1976

Fond memories of Sidney Foster are so many. Passing years have made them seem like a lifetime ago.

It was at one of Bronja and Sidney's wonderful get-togethers in 1975 that I first heard the name of Ernst Schelling. Things were being revealed about this piece of his called *Suite Fantastique for Piano and Orchestra, Op. 7*, written in 1905. Well, the thing that first popped into my mind was "Oh, my god, not another trick question to be possibly asked at my doctoral oral exams!" I thought to myself, "Who in the heck is this composer and why in the world . . . ?!" Soon I was relieved to find that most of the attendees were also clueless as to who, what and why. But not Sidney!

Somehow, and I know not how, Mr. Foster found this dust-covered work that was a potpourri of American folk and patriotic themes – an extravaganza for piano and orchestra. Sidney was excited about this work, not because it was Beethovian in stature, as it surely was not, but because it was an opportunity for him to revive his performing career as we celebrated the 200th anniversary of the birth of our nation. With this piece, Sidney could display his colorful virtuosic pianism and celebrate the bicentennial as well. So Sidney, with his typical fervor and insight, took on the task of resurrecting this long forgotten tour de force.

So as it happened, the concept of performing the Schelling was unfolding and it sparked excitement. Impetuously and without regard to my pecking order, I offered to play the orchestral part for Sidney. No one else jumped at this great opportunity and even more amazing to me, Sidney was interested. Now, I know that any number of my colleagues could have done as well or better, but you know, "the early bird gets . . . !"

It remains a mystery to me as to when Sidney learned the score by himself. To this day, I am convinced that most of his learning of the score was done as I accompanied him in his studio. At this time in his life, Sidney was often not feeling well and not sleeping well. He had a full schedule of students, was the piano chair, and attended most all music school functions. When did he find private time to learn and practice the score?!

About a week passed, and Sidney and I passed in the music school hall in front of Recital Hall, and he gave me a "Xerox" copy of the Schelling score. Charlotte was able to paste the pages back-to-back, to make page-turning easier. (I needed all the help I could get.) She also did this to Sidney's score. I really can't remember how far after that our first reading of the score occurred, but I remember hustling to learn it. The reduction was not really, really hard, but was really, really ineffective. Each time I played it, I would try to reset some parts to make it sound better . . . or maybe sometimes worse. I am sure Sidney noticed these "creative digressions", but without complaint.

The first night we went through the work, I still hadn't a real idea of what it would be like. Not just how the piece went, but what it would be like to accompany my teacher. As I waited in the drab hall by his studio, lit by old ceiling lights and surrounded by icon-like big brown doors, I became anxious and went to look for Mr. Foster at "the circle." There came Sidney, driving up in his massive Olds 98, which he loved dearly. He parked, and I quickly went back and waited near his studio so as not to display my concerns. Soon Sidney turned the corner and walked down the hallway towards me. He was in a dress jacket with loose shirt collar. His slight limp was apparent and he had just combed back his hair with his hand. With his usual wry smile he said, "Harry, I hope I am ready to do this!" I voiced the same feelings about myself as he unlocked and opened the studio door. As we went in, Sidney removed his jacket and took the left Steinway. I immediately sensed he was getting down to his work. He was not fooling around and there was little dialogue between us...only what the music said. Sidney did not play by accident or technical convenience. He played what he heard and the way he heard it might change from day to day.

We continued that routine many late nights. I think this may have been his most convenient practice time, and these sessions were spent playing, or should I say practicing through the Schelling with Sidney. His practice was not like practicing scales for speed or evenness, but was more like the sculpting of sound and color at once. Mr. Foster practiced on the level that he played. There was not a moment of recitation or mindless repetition. Instead, there was a sense of syntax and revelation that was in the moment—it was a feeling of improvisation and re-composition.

As the time came closer to the performance with the Indianapolis Symphony, Bronja joined our nightly get-togethers. As you can imagine, it made me nervous. But Sidney's performance had a refined, polished quality to it, and yet, it seemed as fresh as a newborn. After we finished, Bronja commented on how "interesting" his playing was. I remember Sidney playing one passage over a few times. Now being somewhat perplexed and curious, I asked Sidney, "Why are you playing that passage over, because it already sounds great?" Bronja tried to hush me for my brazen inquisition, but Sidney stopped and explained what he was trying to do—the shape of multiple lines. So I listened as he worked with his sculpture. It made sense! Ah! A lesson!!

Another time, late night of course, Sidney played the Schelling for Zadel Skolovsky, who was also a Curtis friend and at that time was visiting professor at Indiana University. It seemed that the more challenging the audience, the more Sidney rose to the occasion. Sidney enjoyed the performance as well as did Zadel. It was exciting to see Sidney so comfortable in his arena.

One of the last times I accompanied him was a "tryout" performance with Menahem Pressler attending. I can't remember if Charlotte was turning pages that evening, as she did many times. But at any rate, Bronja was there. I wish I had some drugs for anxiety. But, no luck . . . At this point, the Schelling was ready and Sidney was in great command. It was as though he had played it 100 times with the Philadelphia Orchestra. Mr. Foster went to work and played with abandon. Impressive! I was proud of my teacher and was honored to be a small part in the achievement. But as usual I had a couple of "clunkers." This was obviously a result of my desire not to over-practice so as to avoid being stale! (What a laugh!) I still hated the reduction, so I was still trying to make it sound orchestral. As it was, Menahem exuberantly congratulated Sidney on his truly stalwart performance. Afterwards there was a moment of silence. At that point, Mr. Pressler tore into me about my deviations from perfection, and complained of my lack of respect for my teacher that I should make such errors. I explained that I was changing the settings of the orchestral score to more simulate the correct sounds. Then my fatal mistake was to ask him if he would like to try it and make a better substitute. As you can imagine, he became even more incensed and I was sweating it. Quickly Bronja and Sidney came to my rescue and quelled his Napoleonic attack. Whew!!!!!

About a week before the concert, Charlotte and I drove to Indianapolis to hear the first rehearsal. To my horror and others, it was frightful. It seemed the orchestra parts were not in proper sequence, and the orchestra and conductor didn't know the score. At one point, Sidney was playing the horn parts because they were lost and because he had to teach them the score. I thought, "Oh, my god, not this for Sidney. He deserves more!" The orchestra was outclassed. At any rate, the concert happened, Sidney played brilliantly and the orchestra was led by him to a successful conclusion. And deservedly, Sidney got a standing ovation.

As it goes or went, nothing really took off for Sidney with the Schelling. We were all hoping for the spark that could propel his career once more. I know Sidney took it to New York and played it for the powers that were at that time. Sidney did not voice or show cynicism or disappointment after this, as he knew the business of music well.

So the years have passed and 30 years later I talk of Sidney and these things and the way he was. He deserved more. Sidney . . .

IMELDA DELGADO

Reminiscences of My Beloved Mentor

When I think about Sidney Foster, my mentor, I recall inspiring performances he played, advice he gave, food he prepared, incomparable and witty humor, an incredible generosity and a superior intelligence.

I first met and heard Mr. Foster when he performed the Grieg Concerto in Corpus Christi, Texas with the Corpus Christi Symphony Orchestra conducted by Jacques Singer. I was a college student member of that orchestra and eventually a soloist with it. I do not recall what other works were on that evening's concert, but the Grieg—which I also played—was unforgettable!

The slightly built Mr. Foster had a powerful sound that rose above the orchestral *fortissimos*, and all the while playing with an economy of motion without showy gestures. His tone was heartbreakingly beautiful, just perfect for the opening of the second movement and all of the concerto melodies.

Mr. Foster's manner back stage was easy going, approachably friendly. A curious detail that I still visualize is the enormous watch that he wore on his left wrist even while he played.

After that concert I never heard about him until I transferred to Indiana University for graduate study on a Master of Music degree in piano performance. At my audition for him, I played sections of the Chopin G minor Ballade. He was direct and accurately assessed my playing by stating: "You have the quality in your playing that makes people sit up and listen, but your hands and arms are so still that it keeps your sound very small." I explained that I hadn't always played that way but I had been instructed during the past two years to "keep your hands still and fingers always close to the keys so as even a piece of typing paper cannot come between them."

It took two years for me to learn the concepts of technique that are inseparable to the delivery of music through the piano by using Hanon, Czerny, Op. 299, the cumulative scale in D-flat, arpeggios, bouncing exercises, Weber's *Perpetual Motion*, Four Chopin Etudes, and constant reminders to "let go of the keys, loosen your wrist, transfer the weight, up with chords." His persistence and patience got me the joy of playing again and I developed power and a beautiful tone. Once he commented to a listener after I had played in class: "How can those skinny arms produce such power?" Sidney Foster wasn't just a coach, he was an extraordinary teacher!

Living in Bloomington and being under the wing of both Mr. and Mrs. Foster—Bronja and Sidney—was being part of an extended family that observed and absorbed both artistic and human values that changed our lives forever. The Sunday piano classes gave us the venue to try out the repertoire we were learning and the opportunity to learn how to listen critically and comment intelligently about what we heard.

Mr. Foster was both articulate and succinct, and in him, we had an example and a superior role model. Often after recitals or piano class, he would take all of us on picnics to Brown County State Park or his home where much of the time he would prepare gourmet dishes with artichokes and feta cheese or just scrumptious hot dogs and burgers. His tuna melts were popular, and once I got a big charge when he introduced his Baked Alaska which I had never had before!

At these social gatherings, this extended family would witness his quick wit and humor as was the case when once I brought my contribution to a friend's birthday party, a weirdly large cake I'd baked. As he eyed it curiously, I quickly blurted out that "She wanted a big cake," to which he quipped: "Well, this is an interpretation!" So we laughed and then sampled my baking efforts such as they were.

Sidney Foster was of the opinion that there were two types of students he would encounter:

- Those who come to a teacher expecting to be told that what they are doing is good, and
- Those who in essence want to be taught: "Show me, teach me."
- From experience, he also observed two basically different approaches performers had:
- Those who would search the score to find what the composer had intended, what was there, and
- Those who would go to the score with the attitude: "What can I do to it?"

His teaching of so many with varying talents and accomplishments honed his already extraordinary creative ability. He listened critically and demonstrated. His criticism wasn't sugar coated but it wasn't cruel. He was direct, tough, but also fair.

I recall a lesson on the Liszt *Tarantella* when as I arrived at the final statement that builds to a *fortississimo*, I tore into it with all the immature, youthful exaggeration. So he did his job saying: "Imelda, you are banging!" From then on I remembered that the dynamics in good phrasing, every note is NOT played equally loud just as in speaking we don't pronounce each word or syllable with sameness of dynamics.

When we played creatively he offered complimentary comment as was the case the following year when I was learning the Chopin B minor Sonata. As I came to the ending of the exposition of the first movement, he stopped me and said, "The interpretation-*rubato* you played just now in the closing section is most expressive and is something that cannot be taught."

Looking back to those years of piano lessons with this mentor, the realization of all that I learned is incredible. After the initial stages of needing to unlearn limiting technical approaches to piano playing, for the first time I began to understand what was meant by projection: the difference between using a "stage voice" and a "conversational tone," and most critically for music-making on the piano—the concept of "using the keys" as opposed to "playing the keys." We let go of the keys as the composer's intent is for the sound to be held, not the keys.

The advice Sidney Foster gave all of his students, though sometimes unsolicited, was just part of the experience of studying with a person of his caliber. And in the late Fifties and early Sixties, it was particularly valuable to his women students who were contemplating careers in the world of academe. He was aware and concerned about human issues and needs. He made the difference in my landing a college teaching job. Yes, I had earned two academic degrees at first rate universities; yes, I was articulate and attractive; and yes, I was also a woman. When I kept my appointment with a placement agency that set up shop at Indiana School of Music, I was told right up front that I would not get a job because I was a woman. "They want men on their teaching staffs," said the interviewer agent. I related all of this to Mr. Foster. He simply said, "We'll see."

My mentor had influence and he used it wisely. He arranged a private audition for me with Dean Wilfred Bain. I had just played a hearing for the Master's recital and had been nominated for the Performer's Certificate, so he didn't hesitate to put his reputation on the line. The three of us met in the recital hall and, as Dean Bain asked me to play, Mr. Foster told him to ask me for the hardest piece (*Triana* by Albéniz) and a second piece from my recital of his own choosing. I played quite well, and the recommendation he wrote for me—I was later told at my job interview that it was not the usual recommendation that they had read before from Dean Bain—was exceptional. As the Dean of the school he was called to write hundreds of recommendations for faceless forms brought to his desk without the benefit of a special introduction or plea from a major professor. Mr. Foster's action elevated this candidate from the enormous pool of applicants for a very limited job market.

Through the years, I continue to hear his most succinct and sage advice that he gave me at nodal points in my life. "Be creative . . . ! Reach for the stars. Life is what you make it. You have to learn to fit the world because the world is never going to learn to fit you." And when my father died, he said, "Lose yourself in your work, Imelda," and I did, which helped me through my grief. The most significant statement he uttered, however, which has guided me through the decades, and one which reflected his philosophy of life is, "Continue to do things for yourself so that you can continue to do things for others." As mentors go, he was incomparable!

DAVID EFFRON

My dear teacher, Sidney Foster, is never far from my thoughts, especially during the past ten years that I have been a Professor at Indiana University. At least once a day, I pass the studio where the many lessons I took in the years 1960-1962 were—as I discovered later were not only lessons about piano playing and music, but in many ways were more important lessons of human relationships, acceptance of others and models of the teacher-student relationship—a model that I try to pattern myself in the relationship with my own students.

Sidney always thought I was a gifted pianist—in fact, he once had a serious conversation with me about the feasibility of going into some major competitions and doing some concertizing. But my heart was always set on being a conductor with an emphasis on opera. That was pretty logical from my point of view as I knew it was easier than playing the piano at a high level.

How this poor man must have suffered at my lessons when I would come in half prepared although at other times I was able to benefit greatly from Sidney's wisdom as an artist. What I didn't know at the time was that I was being tutored in the lessons of humility, respect for the art form which I had chosen and many a lesson on how to get the best out of an individual by being supportive and at the same time being completely honest.

I loved Sidney as he represented a type of man that I had never experienced. My mentors had always been "Dictator Teachers." They were extremely competent in their expertise but one produced, not out of love, but out of fear. Although at that time my immaturity didn't allow me to understand what many gifts Sidney gave to me, his influence was so strong that many years later I realized that I had been in the presence of not only a great pedagogue and artist, but a man who was able to impart many lessons beyond music.

And, I will never forget his playing—no one played like Sidney—and although I have been in this profession for forty-five years and have worked with many of the great pianists—I have never heard anyone who played with such spontaneity, such creative musical and spiritual ideas, and could hold an audience entranced by the honesty which he brought to music making.

Maybe it is predestined, but when I came back to Bloomington in 1998, I renewed my acquaintance with Bronja and Justin. I didn't know Bronja well as a student, but I did spend many an evening with the Fosters because their home was always open to all of us. That unusual relationship between teacher and students actually strengthened the respect that we all had for the Foster family. I remember feeling that I had a safe haven at their home, a moment's repose from my self-created tumultuous life.

CARLISLE FLOYD

I first met Sidney in the fall of 1949 when he joined the faculty of Florida State University, where I had returned to re-join the same faculty after a year's leave to get a master's degree. It seems to me that we quickly became friends and I do know that Don Rand (a good friend of mine who had just come on the Florida State University faculty also) and I were regular visitors in Sidney's and Bronja's home, becoming extended family very shortly and we remained close friends for as long as the Fosters were in Tallahassee. As was also the case at Indiana University, I imagine, the Fosters (principally Sidney) were inveterate party givers and the parties could be spur of the moment occasions or planned ones but more often the former. I remember Sidney's meeting me at the door when I was late arriving at one of their announced parties and, with his wicked sense of humor, saying "Carlisle, I'm so glad you're here: this is the kind of party I'd leave if I weren't giving it!"

After a recital I played early in the fall semester of 1949, I asked Sidney for his reaction and he responded by saying that nobody really wants to hear an objective opinion from a friend. I was a little surprised by such directness but managed nevertheless to convince him that I really wanted to know. The response that I got (and had asked for) was, to put it kindly, not complimentary. A little taken aback, I nonetheless took his evaluation seriously and subsequently asked if I could have some lessons with him. Although I was a colleague, if only twenty three, he agreed with the understanding that I would be willing to start over technically from the beginning and thus I began the familiar standard Foster overhaul. Although I had a master's degree in piano and had performed with orchestra I had privately faced the fact that I was in need of technical help, so I willingly accepted his conditions.

Thus began the relentless but patient and uncompromising training that was his style of teaching which eventually transformed my playing and made it possible for me to become the pianist I had hoped to be. Although I worked with Sidney for only the better part of a semester it was by far the most important time I ever spent with a mentor: he was that rare combination of a teacher in the best sense of the word, and at the same time an insightful and articulate coach. I will always be indebted to him, not only for the invaluable technical work, but also he expanded and illuminated my musical thinking in such a way that it really provided the touchstone for all of my musical growth since.

In addition to all this he and Bronja were the kind of friends one treasures for life and even after all these years I still love them and miss them.

J.B. FLOYD

Sidney Foster and His Legacy

We are fortunate during our life span, especially the earlier, formative years, to be blessed with teachers or mentors who transform us in important ways that have a lasting effect. One such important person in my life was certainly Sidney Foster.

Another mentor guided me to him—Maestro Jacques Singer—the distinguished conductor and brother-in-law of Mr. Foster. The year was 1955 when I heard a remarkable performance by Sidney of the Grieg Piano Concerto, conducted by Maestro Singer with the Corpus Christi Symphony. I immediately wanted to study with this man and entered the D.M. program in performance at Indiana University in 1956.

I was 26-years-old, had been teaching at universities since 1949 and had played a debut recital at the Town Hall, New York City, in 1952. I was eager for musical guidance and found my lessons from the very first day with Mr. Foster to be revelatory. Here was a great artist who had a natural affinity for the piano but who had a complete understanding of the physical mechanics necessary for technical mastery based on an economy of effort. Sidney was able to analyze quickly the multitude of technical problems that individual students encounter and to effectively alleviate and eliminate the root causes. This he did day after day and always with great interest, patience and encouragement.

I became a much better technician because of his understanding of my problems, his persistence in solving them, and when I would be discouraged, his constant encouragement. Moreover, I became a much better musician because of his complete understanding of the art of making music. He opened my eyes and ears to formal structure, thematic contrast and the art of making the smallest musical phrase come to life as if by magic.

If this description seems to imply a pedagogical prescription for making music by "coloring within the lines" or methodology over spontaneous expression, this would be a gross misrepresentation of Sidney Foster the artist and the teacher. Above all Sidney taught and lived with the desire for spontaneity. Music made according to the circumstances of the moment. The way that one begins a piece determines the pathway that leads the performer to its ultimate expression.

Mr. Foster instilled the adventure of spontaneity in performance in all of his students that caused us to be intensely engaged in the re-creation of a composition. He was amazingly generous to everyone he came in contact with: abundant with his time, hospitality and support of every kind. He loved company and entertained with his wife Bronja regularly. He continued to live a "New York City" schedule in Bloomington, Indiana, retiring after three a.m. and beginning his day in the afternoon. I remember many lessons I had that began at midnight. He had a terrific sense of humor. One example: before one of my New York recitals, he sent a telegram "Happy landings, especially to each finger."

I will always be grateful for the valuable and pleasurable time I was able to spend with this man, his wife, Bronja, and his two sons, Lincoln and Justin, and he will always be over my shoulder when I perform or teach.

HELENA FREIRE (BRAZIL)

The Fosters and I

It is a great honor and pleasure to write about Professor Sidney Foster and how he changed my pianistic and professional life. A long time ago, when I arrived at the School of Music at Indiana University, I had my pianistic development almost completed. I used to play concerts and participated in many competitions in my country, Brazil.

During my master's degree at Indiana University, I felt at that time that I was not improving my piano playing as I expected. To be admitted into Mr. Foster's piano class was a big hope for me, and when that happened, he asked me, "Do you really want to change your piano technique and be submitted to what I will ask you to do?" "Yes!" was my answer.

Since that day I had to reformulate the basics at the piano. In the following six months Hanon and Czerny were my only repertoire. A new philosophy and technique were focused with a variety of speed and approaches. In fact they were really hard, but very productive for gaining a musical perspective.

One day Mr. Foster said, "Now it is time to learn how to use the three pedals." The Chopin Prelude, Op. 45 (1841), was our target. As a "magic step" I saw my performance development and technique revealed as a "Foster's stamp." Ever since that really hard time, I have been using the three pedals in my playing and in teaching my students.

What I learned with Mr. Foster is something so great, and it is easily recognized in my piano playing with a variety of composers and repertoire. These attributes are beautiful colors and magnificent sound, as well as marvelous musical concepts.

Mr. and Mrs. Foster opened their home to me and my colleagues on many occasions with warm affection which was very important for our growth as human beings. During my studies, Mr. Foster took care of me as a part of his family. He demonstrated that by taking me for health treatment with his medical doctor, Dr. Holtzman.

I am very grateful for what he did for my musical growth and piano playing. In fact, when Sidney Foster left, my heart felt empty without his presence, but full of joy with respect for life and music making. All his goals for me were completed by my dearest Bronja. She helped me gain the security for the technical approach as a key for more expressive music making.

In the last twenty years I have been working as a full Associate Professor at the School of Music of the Federal University of Minas Gerais, in Belo Horizonte, Brazil. I have to recognize that Sidney Foster with his teaching helped me to achieve excellence in my piano playing.

MIRIAM GARGARIAN

Tribute to Sidney Foster

Regardless of physical size of body and hand, whether undergraduate or doctoral candidate, the students of Sidney Foster played with ease, with clear intention, and with beautiful tone quality. This was my observation as a new student in his studio in the summer of 1967. I was privileged to study with him until his death in 1977. In retrospect I can appreciate with greater understanding that Mr. Foster nurtured artistry in three ways: technically, intellectually, and psychologically. He was able to discuss piano technique in objective terms believing that the purpose of technique was to serve the musical thought. As important as finger technique, was the skillful use of pedaling to create textures of sound. Few pianists have a master of pedaling like Sidney had. Listening to him play was like watching a great painter apply paint to canvas. He used the pedals in myriads of combinations to heighten the desired effect of his masterful fingers.

Sidney challenged each student to create a "point of view" or "opinion" of the music based upon detailed study of the score. The concept that great music did not have one ideal interpretation, but could lend itself to different equally-valid interpretations was liberating indeed! Every performance became an opportunity to recreate the score. He expressed himself verbally with the same eloquence that he did musically. He taught me how to think like a composer so that interpretive decisions became purposeful, relevant, and spontaneous.

Every Sunday afternoon the Foster students met from two to four p.m. in the recital hall to perform for each other and to comment on the performances. The atmosphere was one of camaraderie. It was fascinating to hear different, sometimes diametrically opposed, reactions to the same performance. This performance laboratory not only nurtured artistic performance, it also nurtured critical listening and articulate verbal discussion of music. Sidney was correct that these afternoons would benefit his students in the future as performers and as teachers. He was extremely generous with his time, listening to his students collectively and privately in the recital hall.

Mr. Foster preferred to be addressed simply as Sidney. My admiration for him was so great that I did so with difficulty. He once said, "Think of me as a more experienced colleague." He was a great pianist, a person of impeccable integrity, and a delightful wit. If I were to choose one word to describe how Sidney taught, that word would be "empowerment." Sidney empowered his students technically, intellectually, and psychologically to become artists in their own right.

HERBERT GOLUB

At a memorial service in 1962 for Dr. Vincent Jones of the New York University Department of Education, who had been my mentor in college, I met a former classmate who had recently completed a doctorate at Indiana. He mentioned Sidney Foster as an important member of the piano faculty there. I was familiar with his work. I wanted to pursue another degree beyond the master's so my wife, Ina, and I decided to leave our teaching jobs to attend graduate school in Bloomington.

The hour of my audition with Sidney loomed as I nervously paced the hall outside his studio. He finally invited me in and I saw a slight man with piercing black eyes, a shock of grey hair reminiscent of Beethoven's, and a gentle but serious smile. I played the Schumann *Carnaval* and after a few pages he stopped me to point out some technical flaws in my technique including how tight my body was as I sat at the keyboard. He reassuringly said he could help me and invited me to join his graduate class of piano students. This was rather unusual as I had been accepted into Indiana University as a Music Education major and he worked mostly with performance majors. Little did I know that September evening that my encounter with Sidney Foster would change my life.

For me, Sidney presented a new viewpoint toward performing and listening–and teaching. He completely renovated my piano technique and thus changed my attitude toward music forever. He gave me a whole new concept of teaching which I later carried home to New Jersey and to my students at Kean University, where I was on the music faculty from 1965 to 2004 when I retired.

My first lesson with Sidney Foster focused on the Hanon first exercise. He taught me how to support my weight and drop my wrists at the same time. For countless hours in the practice room I held my head high and my wrists low and for years afterward, I taught my piano students to do the same. I studied with Sidney for two years, attending his exciting evening and Sunday afternoon piano classes with fellow graduate students, often followed by a meal in a local restaurant or provided by his wife at home along with lots of conversation about life. I came away from that experience with a new fire in my playing kindled by my mentor.

But that was not all!

Sidney and his wife, Bronja, their sons Justin and Lincoln, and their dachshund, Paddyfoot, welcomed Sidney's students into their lives. Ina and I ate sumptuous meals at their home on many occasions including our first Thanksgiving in Bloomington, when all the guests were folks who, for one reason or another, couldn't leave the campus for the holiday. There were picnics in a nearby park, parties after piano class, and other social activities. All this led to a new philosophy of teaching when I was hired in Kean University in New Jersey. For over thirty five years, I taught an evening class in Music History on a different topic each semester. I initiated a dinner break during the sessions, directly influenced by Foster, which created a highly social atmosphere and provided an optimal learning atmosphere. The university population clamored to register for this class and many returned year after year.

Sidney Foster was quite the performer. On a Sunday afternoon in the winter of 1963, Ina and I heard him play Rachmaninoff's Rhapsody at Clowes Hall in Indianapolis. He played according to his principles which displayed his musical viewpoint and technical wizardry. We also heard him show his genius again at Carnegie Hall in New York in December of 1966. In the early 70's I went back to Bloomington to have Sidney critique Beethoven's Emperor Concerto which I was preparing to perform with a New Jersey orchestra. As diminutive as he was in stature, that's how huge his heart was. Each student was treated as an individual with great love and consideration.

On that visit in the 70's, however, Ina and I noticed a change in Sidney's demeanor. We felt there was a weakness we hadn't noticed before and he appeared pale, yet he was just as caring and giving as ever and Bronja prepared a lovely repast one evening during our stay. Not too many months later we had news that he was desperately ill. His family took him to Tufts University in Boston for treatment. The extended family of students had a phone relay to keep each other informed about his condition. By the time Veda Zuponcik reached us to tell us our beloved mentor had died we had already seen the obituary in the New York Times. When Ina opened the paper on February 8, 1977, already heavy of heart expecting sad news any time, she burst into tears at the breakfast table. She too was under the spell of a great human being.

ROBERT HAMILTON

Sidney Foster was my piano teacher during the formative undergraduate years (1955-1959), and again in the late 1960's after I had accepted a newly created artist position at Indiana University South Bend (my home town). I considered Sidney a good friend as well, particularly in our latter period when I sometimes sought his counsel. My gratitude to him is considerable, and will be expressed in three general categories: His instruction and living example as a pianist, his power and inspiration as a personality, and his generosity.

When I arrived in the fall of 1955, Mr. Foster had developed his own method that, perhaps, grew in part from his studies with Isabelle Vengerova and David Saperton at Curtis. Although my early instruction centered on technique, it also incorporated a number of very helpful phrasing principles (such as 2-3-4-ONE). He taught me a number of skills, such as using the damper pedal to create legato lines in place of the fingers (he often said the piano should be used more like an open harp, with dampers free of the strings except when changes were needed—just the reverse of the usual understanding and approach).

A key ingredient of his work with students at the time was the cure of what might be termed "wrong note phobia." More than once I recall being encouraged outright to strike wrong notes, just so I would not stiffen in attempts to hit the right ones. It was not unusual for him to join into the "wrong note feast" at the other piano, chiming in with a number of his own. At such times

I could only wonder what fellow students walking by at my lesson time might think. He often told me: "If you're going to hit a wrong note, make it a bold one." (Being a Lutheran, this reminded me of Martin Luther's advice to be unafraid of living and to "sin boldly.") Finally, as was Sidney's custom, the *Perpetual Motion* movement of the C major Sonata by Weber was assigned to me—a piece I have never heard anyone perform with the dash and excitement of our teacher. I believe I may have been given a few Czerny exercises, but remember distinctly that he liked only the *School of Velocity* at the time (and not the *Art of Finger Dexterity*, whose complexity he believed stripped those particular exercises of useful merit). All of this occurred in the first semester, during which time I was asked to avoid playing previously learned pieces, lest older approaches and tensions interfere with fundamental changes we were pursuing. By the end of the second semester of my freshman year I felt like a new pianist, and quite ably performed the Tchaikovsky First Piano Concerto with a couple of community orchestras.

Before venturing off campus to perform the Tchaikovsky with orchestras, I played it in Recital Hall with Sidney at my side on the second piano. Once we were seated onstage, he startled me by calmly offering a Lifesaver mint—right in front of the audience. It did help to settle the nerves, and I recall a performance of newfound ease, successfully exhibiting what I had been shown. It also unveiled one of the principles of our teacher: to establish complete comfort and relaxation in performance, whatever the cost. He himself was always absolutely at home and totally in command onstage. His personality and (for me) masculine approach to performing free from excessive emotionalism or fancy key manipulations – delighted and instructed us all, as he was the ideal embodiment of everything that he taught. Teachers often fall short of demonstrating the totality of what they teach in the heat of public performance. Not Sidney. He had us all so convinced by the teaching and onstage display of his ways that I recall on many occasions criticizing otherwise fine touring pianists who did not happen to incorporate his principles. This was not chiefly due to the customary impressionableness of young people; Sidney had an uncommon ability to dominate and persuade.

Our teacher's personality was absolutely unique. With a twinkle in the eyes, raised voice and typical cock of the head, he seemed to love life and living with an enthusiasm that was contagious. While customarily respectful and cooperative in public, he could also sharply stand up for principles that he believed in. I will give two examples. The wonderful yearly school piano competitions, for the privilege of performing with the Indiana University Symphony Orchestra (undoubtedly established through Sidney's persuasiveness with the Dean), were attended by an audience seated in the balcony. On one occasion it was felt by the judges—a distinguished faculty group including Willi Apel, among others,—that the crowd upstairs was just too noisy. After brief discussion, one of them publicly announced that the audience must leave. With some grumbling, people began to exit. Sidney, who happened to be seated upstairs among us, immediately stood up and, in his distinctive voice, gave a short but piercing response to their decision which, he said, would unavoidably establish a climate of suspicion surrounding the results. Competitions should be open, he declared, admonishing his colleagues to reconsider. Within minutes we were back in our seats. A second example comes by way of a friend, former Indiana University-South Bend Fine Arts Dean Robert W. Demaree, Jr., who in this capacity attended faculty council meetings in Bloomington. In his words:

At one of our Academic Council meetings—made up of department heads and administrators, and chaired by Dean Bain—a large group of the Council members presented a proposal to (finally) provide secretarial support to a School of Music faculty in excess of 150. Distinguished individuals like Sidney, Joseph Gingold, János Starker, Willi Apel and Paul Nettl were handwriting, typing or paying outsiders to type their professional correspondence. One after another of the Council members spoke strongly in favor of the proposal until Bain asked: 'Where am I to find the money for these two new secretaries? I have no unallocated funds. Shall I take it from your salaries?' There was an uncomfortable and lengthy silence. Then Sidney spoke up: 'Well, you may begin with my salary': A surprised Bain said: 'Alright, who else will volunteer?' At this point there was an even longer silence, after which Bain continued: 'Moving on to the next item on our agenda . . . ' This dramatic, stand-alone contribution of Foster was typical. At the same time, he was forever eloquent and graceful, with a command of the English language I regarded to be Churchillian in scope. He was undeniably the most well-spoken colleague I have ever served with.

Sidney was known to retire to bed quite late at night, apparently practicing from midnight until around 3:00 a.m. Three hours a day was, incidentally, the outer limit he considered appropriate for practice, and he would discourage students when he suspected they were practicing longer than that.

Sidney Foster exuded an aura of complete professionalism, which brought the respect and trust of his many colleagues, including Dean Bain. He was personally responsible for the faculty acquisitions of Abbey Simon and Jorge Bolet. I never knew him to permit differences with other faculty to invade his customary gentlemanly demeanor, and in my presence, he always referred to his colleagues with the utmost respect.

Sidney always urged his students to express themselves and speak out verbally at master classes following the performances of fellow students. At first some of us found this difficult, but with time each of us became quite proficient.

Finally, Sidney is one of the most generous persons I have encountered in music. All of us greatly treasured the many fabulous parties which he and Bronja threw for us at their home, or at an area park, and so forth. He was always free with his time, and wouldn't hesitate to spend valuable moments conversing with us on a wide variety of topics. Whenever I was getting ready for an important degree recital or off-campus concert, I could count always on more than the expected listening time from my teacher. Perhaps his most surprising act of generosity towards me came as I was preparing to leave Bloomington in 1959. At the time there was a military draft. On the advice of many (including Sidney), I had elected to continue in the ROTC program during my junior and senior years, to take on a commission as an officer in the Army, and to return to Indiana University for a master's degree following the required six months of active duty.

Just months away from accepting my commission, I heard of the US Army Band and Chorus in Washington, D.C., and of their need for a pianist. I auditioned and got the position, which set entirely different plans into motion. I was now to be on active duty for three full years, in Washington where I would rehearse just two hours daily besides performing several "jobs" at the State Department each week, as well as playing concerts. I was to have lots of wonderful spare time to begin a professional career, and of course to continue my piano studies. Rather than to simply send me off with the customary "good luck" and "I'll see you back here in three years," Sidney went to bat finding me a teacher on the east coast. His number one choice was Vladimir Horowitz, whom he asked to consider taking me. I was instructed to telephone Mr. Horowitz on a Tuesday night at precisely 9:45 to set up an audition with him. When I called, I was told that Mr. Horowitz had retired early, and to call again the next Tuesday. After several such calls, the appointment was set and I played my entire senior recital for him in his home. He coached me on the pieces and, while seemingly impressed, informed me that he was soon to leave for six months in Europe, during which time he would think about taking me as his student. I told Sidney that I didn't want to wait, at which point he put me in touch with Leon Fleisher at Peabody. I well remember Fleisher's comment after hearing me: "Crazy! You don't need me, you need management," suggesting that I contact Columbia Artists.

Sidney next put me in touch with Abram Chasins, who had studied with Hoffman and Rachmaninoff among others. Chasins heard me, and wanted to pawn me off on his wife, Constance Keene, which did not please Sidney at all. Finally, he said, "Well, Abbey has studied with Dora Zaslavsky of the Manhattan School, and speaks very highly of her; maybe you should give her a try." I did, and she became my coach over the ensuing eight years, during which time I won many awards and launched my performing career here and abroad. Still I always felt it was primarily Sidney's teaching that had provided me with the necessary tools for success, and his selfless interest in my future and career as I left Bloomington is something I will always remember.

In his book *The Art of Piano Playing*, Heinrich Neuhaus writes perceptibly about the conflict of the performing ("artist") teacher:

When a teacher is also a performer . . . it is natural that his teaching work should be carried on differently from that of "pure" teachers who never appear on the concert platform. It frequently occurred to me that, though the teacher-performer offers a number of undoubted advantages compared to one who is a teacher only—and first of all the advantage of being a living example—yet to a certain extent, one who is purely a teacher appears in a way to be more of one piece. His life and profession seem unwaveringly directed at a single aim merely because, to put it bluntly, he has never had to sit on two chairs. He devotes himself entirely to his pupils, and only to his pupils, demanding nothing for himself. If a performer is overtaken with teaching work he is conscious at every moment of the harm which this excessive workload causes to his favorite occupation, that of performing. And even if this awareness does not have a negative effect on his teaching, it inevitably affects his morale.

I can say with complete honesty that I was never—not once—even distantly aware of any such conflict in Sidney's life, though it surely existed. More than anyone else I have known, he steadfastly conveyed the image of one totally absorbed and happy in the disparate sides of his work. Students are quick in sensing when their teacher's concern is more for his own playing and career than for their instruction. That we never experienced this feeling with Sidney, while he continually maintained his high performance level as our "living example" was, I believe, truly remarkable. I salute him as a rare embodiment of the near Impossible: Artist Performer and Teacher Par Excellence!

ALAN HERSH

Sidney

I left military service in September, 1965, to attend graduate school at Indiana University. After a year of confusion and frustration with the Artist Teacher with whom I had chosen to study, I decided to play for Sidney Foster. Mr. Foster agreed to take me as a student once I had made the proper political moves to sever my ties with my current teacher.

When I finished my degree in the summer of 1971, I asked Sidney why more people did not think and teach as he did. His ideas about music and piano technique were so carefully thought out, presented, and explained, that it seemed to me only indifference kept everyone from knowing and doing the same. I was a true believer. Sidney said, "People know what they want to know." I have recalled this farewell gift many times since then, and recognized both the truth and sadness of this profound insight. "People know what they want to know." Most of us have too much baggage to be willing to cut to the heart of the matter and be attentive to what needs tending.

Sidney Foster was the first piano instructor in my experience who had a completely thought out method of developing the physical aspect of piano playing. All of his students did similar kinds of exercises and repertoire, chosen to develop ease and flexibility at the keyboard. Sidney held that a pianist's musical ideas were dictated by his/her technical capacity and comfort. Often an unmusical performance was a performance in which the pianist made compromises necessitated by technical insufficiency. "You can only play as well as you can play," he said, or something similar to that. That was why he insisted that every pianist learn the technical "craft" of piano playing, even before he worried about their artistic development. Since many of his former students hold positions in colleges and universities throughout the world, many of his teaching ideas have become widespread.

Sidney brought to the study of music the same clarity of thought and understanding that he brought to technique. He was a fabulous pianist, perhaps the greatest Beethoven pianist I have ever heard. He also played Schumann with consummate understanding. Indeed, his repertoire spanned the Common Practice Period and extended well into the 20th century.

I would describe Sidney's musical approach as "structural." He always believed the composer, by the arrangement of notes, told you how the piece should go. Discovering the patterns and permutations of the music, and creating a performance out of one's discoveries became an odyssey of musical exploration, an invigorating search for the riddle of the musical story. Coupled with the technical clarity that made playing physically easy, this approach to piano study was like rediscovering the instrument. The "Foster method" is what I and the myriad of "Fosterkind" have tried to incorporate in our own careers as pianists and teachers.

EDWARD J. KAIZER

A Few Thoughts on Sidney Foster and His Influence

Sidney Foster was one of the international pianists whose ability to execute in solo and collaborative roles exceeded his public recognition. He also possessed the ability to educate, and that made him an important contributor to the entire music scene.

These words are my interpretation of Abram Chasins' description of a whole generation of inspiring artists and teachers in his book, *Speaking of Pianists*. It was Chasins who first led me to arrange an audition with Sidney to see if he would take me on as a doctoral student. I remember that as a young athlete, I wasn't sure that this short, slender man with penetrating brownish colored eyes could possibly muster the physical strength to play piano with the sound and technique I thought necessary in an excellent pianist.

That first impression changed drastically, however, when we went into his studio and at one point in my playing he demonstrated a few other musical possibilities in the Schumann piece we were discussing. He presented his ideas with total command of the keyboard, with flawless execution, with an enormous sound, and yet with an apology nonetheless because, "I haven't played this in a long time." While first watching him play in his effortless manner, I vowed I would do whatever necessary to attempt to play with that same level of command and musical intelligence.

During the years that followed, he was able to develop my abilities as a pianist into those of a functioning artist-teacher. I was just one of many Liza Doolittle stories, and as I became more accustomed to the Foster, technique, I became a 'Fosterite'* (all of us believing that "You can't make music until you can technically play the notes").

Being Sidney's student was like getting a key that gives you access to the most divine and profound thoughts in the music before you. The key was that first step of technical command that Sidney made available to us, a step that with his guidance led us to our own personal projection of the composer's profound concepts and emotions.

A key characteristic of Sidney's great teaching was his emphasis on musical communication (appropriate to each compositional style) through the various nuances of sound, articulation, tempo, etc. During my studies with Sidney, I observed that many students respected him for his teaching of technique yet failed to realize that his teaching of musical concepts (reflecting all aspects of the music being studied) was the more definitive aspect of his greatness as a teacher.

I thank Sidney every time I have a student I can assist in developing his or her pianistic, or more broadly, musical abilities so that they can discover the ideas and emotions expressed in the many great piano compositions. Each of us Fosterites has his or her unique ways in which we pass along Sidney's relaxed technique and musical concepts to our students. And I believe that the world and the entire musical scene are richer due to the many Fosterites who now make up an integral part of our collective musical heritage.

Certainly, the personal experience of learning from and knowing Sidney, his wife Bronja, and his children Justin and Lincoln have enriched and shaped my life as a musician and as a person. For that opportunity, I will be forever grateful.

Fosterite: A student who has been enriched by the musical and non-musical impact of the great pedagogue, Sidney Foster. This includes not only the first-generations (those Sidney taught directly), but also the later generations who are the students of students.

CHIU-LING LIN

I attended Indiana University from 1970 to 1975, as a master's and doctoral student after receiving my undergraduate degree from New England Conservatory of Music. I was very much a foreign student back then – born in Taiwan, growing up in Singapore. During my pre-college years, I received a Chinese education and learned English as a second language. This background, and my personal shyness, is what I brought with me to Mr. Foster as a first year graduate student. Unlike most students, I did not have any personal "connection" with him through former teachers prior to my arrival on the Bloomington campus. Somehow, he took me in as his twenty-fifth student on a January day in 1970. To this day, it still puzzles me how and why this happened. I only know deep in my heart that this good fortune changed my life and began a brand new journey for me as a pianist.

During the course of my five years at Indiana University, little did I know that Mr. Foster would become a major force in molding me to become stronger both as a pianist and as a teacher. His influence on my piano playing not only expanded my technical facility, but also broadened my horizons to understand any kind of music, with a keen sense of what constitutes convincing interpretation. First, it was through the teaching of his technique that I was freed of the tension that so often impeded my small hands. This gave me the power to achieve a warmer and heartier tone without any force. It also became the perfect tool for bolder projection of tonal gradations.

Secondly, I learned about phrasing from understanding the structure of music inside out. Mr. Foster never asked me to imitate him, but instead, invited me to be part of the thinking process of deciding how to play in a certain way. His communication with me was always clear. He sometimes used words that seemed "big" to a student like me, but helped increase my musical vocabulary. His choice of words was always "to the point", however, and never intimidating. I can never forget all the analogies and metaphors he used during those precious lessons. To this day, I often find myself using them in my own teaching.

His impact on my teaching career has been immense. The manner in which he articulated ideas and thoughts were crystal clear. I later realized that a teacher's ability to convey concepts relies on all types of communication skills. Many teachers are successful in demonstrating by performance, but not so articulate verbally. Mr. Foster was eloquent in both. His words were vivid, humorous, and sharp, and his demonstrations were vibrant and colorful. Furthermore, he showed me many principles for interpreting music from different time periods.

As an example of Mr. Foster's gift of teaching, I can never forget learning the art of *rubato* playing from the Chopin B minor Sonata, in preparation for my master's degree recital. At my young age, I thought I could achieve excitement and inspiration just from listening to other pianist's recordings. Little did I know that this shortcut only results in unconvincing performances, without in-depth knowledge. Mr. Foster forced me to obtain insight by learning the phrase structure and form of each piece. Realizing the importance of this process was a major breakthrough in the way I looked at music from that point onward.

Mr. Foster taught me how to think for myself. In doing so, he showed me how ideas can be formulated through various ways of interpretation. I learned from him that true artistry only comes from the artist's integrity and sincerity, and never through mimicry, pretense, or showmanship. He was a champion of genuine originality, and his dedication to his students was also unmatched. He was generous with his time to a fault. Frequently, his lessons would last till midnight. His parties for his students were always memorable, not only as fun-filled times, but as showcases for his culinary skills.

Mr. Foster, more than anything else, was encouraging and inspiration for me. I will always remember how he gave me the motivation and confidence to participate in the 1976 Leventritt Competition, of which he was a laureate as the first prizewinner in 1940. Under his tutelage, I also participated in the 1975 Chopin International Competition in Warsaw. The process and preparation and the experiences I gained from these two prestigious competitions were definitely highlights of my years at Indiana University.

Mr. Foster is the cornerstone of music as a lifelong adventure for me. His influence on my career in performance and teaching persists to this day, and I am truly blessed with the honor and privilege of passing his legacy on to future generations of music students.

THOMAS MASTROIANNI

Sidney Foster, an outstanding musical mind and a pianist of supreme artistry, was known for the beauty and Romantic quality of his pianistic tone. In my study with him in the late 60's, I was constantly impressed by his ability to get to the heart of the musical issues and to impart the skills needed to produce beauty of sound. His technique was so effortless that it permitted him to concentrate on a quality of sound that many pianists of the present generation do not achieve. His use of weight and thrust resembles Liszt's concept of "retropulsion" as described by Bertrand Ott in his book on the *Liszt et la Pedagogie du Piano (Pedagogy of Liszt)*. However, Saperton was surely more directly influential in this approach.

Foster was not only a great pianist and teacher, but a truly exceptional human. He treated his students as colleagues and friends. His warm personality and humor were always present and ready to be shared. He spent endless hours teaching - sometimes well beyond midnight. I recall a lesson that began after midnight, followed by a meal which ended just before 4:00 a.m. This kind of schedule was not unusual for him.

On one occasion, Dean Bain asked him if he would teach the Romantic Piano Seminar - certainly his area of expertise. The class was scheduled to meet at 7:30 a.m. each week. He looked at Dean Bain thoughtfully and asked for some time to consider the request. He returned promptly with a plea that he be excused from this assignment saying "I don't think that I can stay up that late."

I recall with great admiration, the wonderful concerts he played and am deeply grateful for the substantial contribution he made to my own development as a pianist, as a teacher and as a person.

CARYL MATTHEWS

Sidney Foster was soloist with the Indianapolis Symphony Orchestra in 1955 while I was a student at Butler University. When I heard him play, I knew that I had to study with him. I transferred to Indiana University, arriving in January 1956 and learned that Mr. Foster was recuperating from a heart attack. In my naiveté, it never occurred to me that I should contact him to see if he was taking new students. By June, Mr. Foster returned to teaching and, to this day, I count myself most fortunate to have been taken into his studio—and life. He was (and continues to be) the person who most influenced my life as a musician. Just as importantly, beyond my parents, Mr. Foster gave me many wonderful life lessons. He was my teacher, my mentor and my confidante.

Life lessons learned from Mr. Foster: Your family is most important. He counseled me through a very difficult family medical problem and taught me how to handle my emotional distress. When his mother was ill, he left campus the week before one of my recitals, but I knew why he went. Besides, Bronja kept me on a steady course. One of my favorite quotes from Mr. Foster was on preparing for crises: "Don't cross your bridges before you get there, but it's wise to study the map and know some alternate routes if the bridge is closed when you get there."

Mr. Foster's students became part of his family. I remember many wonderful after-recital parties at their home. I attended Indiana University when the women had to "sign out" of the dorm in the evening and be back by 11 p.m. or receive a dreaded pink late slip. Mr. Foster probably held the record for most female students with late slips!

I came to Indiana University as a reasonable pianist and Mr. Foster gave me the technical tools and musical direction to become much more than I ever thought I could. *Perpetual Motion* was my companion for three years and he would ask for it at the oddest times. Hanon and scales with the "onesies, twosies and foursies" still start my piano days. And he was such a master of people psychology—he always knew which button to push to make me unwittingly prove something to myself. For example, one day he made an offhand remark that I was a slow learner. I took great offense at that and went out and learned a Liszt Hungarian Rhapsody over the weekend. I marched in to his studio the next week and handed him the music. It was not a flawless performance—but he had made his point.

Looking back at his markings in some of my music, I find a minimum of directions. But they were really universal kinds of directions, and I carry the results of many of those marks with me to this day. Perhaps that's what makes a "Sidney Foster Student"—giving us the framework (and technique) in which to express ourselves. We certainly did not all sound like each other. In fact, three of us were unwittingly his guinea pigs when he assigned the same piece to us and then had us play it in the Sunday class. Apparently a colleague had said that all his students sounded alike. That person should have been there on that Sunday afternoon—three very different, but valid, performances!

Those Sunday classes in Recital Hall were invaluable. What a teaching time! And when I left the university, I realized how much time he had given us! He taught us how to think critically—and positively. "You can't just say you like it—or dislike it. You have to tell us WHY." HOW to listen critically was a tool that came out of those classes.

That May 1959 graduation was not the end of my relationship with Mr. Foster. I continued lessons sporadically and had opportunities to hear him perform in Columbia, Missouri, Springfield, Missouri, and again with the Indianapolis Symphony Orchestra. Each performance was another inspiration for me. In one of our post-college chats, he asked me when I was going to start calling him Sidney. I don't know if he didn't like it that it was always "Mr. Foster and Bronja" or rather that he felt he had completed his job with me. (He always said that the goal of good teachers was to teach themselves out of a job.) In my heart, he will always be Mister Foster.

JOE MATTHEWS

Remembrances of Sidney Foster

I will never forget my first meeting with Sidney Foster. Dick Morris, my teacher at the University of Missouri and a former student of Mr. Foster, brought me to Bloomington to audition for him. His eyes were the first thing I noticed about Sidney Foster – his penetrating eyes emitted great warmth and intelligence. Right away one felt his sincere personal interest in you the individual, and it was exciting to be in his presence. I feel certain that I did not play well that day, but Mr. Foster's straight forward and unusually perceptive analysis of my performance reinforced my great desire to study with him.

Unfortunately for me, Sidney Foster was on a tour of Russia during my first semester at Indiana University, and my ambition to be one of his students had to be placed on hold. I was extremely lucky, however, in having the opportunity to join the class of the eminent virtuoso and pedagogue Abbey Simon, who also happened to be a close friend of the Fosters. Later, when Mr. Simon took a sabbatical, I was thrilled to receive the opportunity to study with Foster.

No matter how old you were—and I was a graduate student at the time—Mr. Foster devoted the first weeks of study introducing his own technical system. The principles of technique, such as the use of arm weight and the particular coordination of finger, wrist, forearm, and upper arm to achieve specific musical effects, were introduced through five-finger patterns, Hanon studies, Czerny etudes, and ultimately the etudes of major composers. The final movement from von Weber's *Sonata No. 1 in C major*—the-Rondo (*Perpetual Motion*)—was an important milestone in Mr. Foster's technical regimen.

As a teacher, Mr. Foster accomplished what we all aspire to achieve in teaching—he gave his students independence. For example, he taught a method of analyzing the structure of each piece studied. From Mr. Foster I learned that it is imperative for the performer to achieve a comprehensive understanding of the structure in order to convey the meaning of the music. This provided also a way to synthesize one's own personal feelings about the music, and thus create a more powerful performance. With this approach, Mr. Foster encouraged his students to be creative with dynamics and timing, and helped to clarify what aspects of the performance should be personal. Thinking and creating were important components of his teaching. One always left a lesson with much to contemplate and much to achieve in the following practice sessions.

The performances of Sidney Foster were a fascinating and revealing complement to the lessons. They were eloquent and beautiful demonstrations of what he taught. Rich, round tone exposing the optimal beauty of the piano was matched only by the incisive intelligence of the performances. His playing was so persuasive and revealing that one felt as though the music was being heard for the first time.

With his students, Mr. Foster was interested in the "whole" person. It was delightful to converse with him about music as well as many topics outside of music. Although one could be intimidated by his enormous talent and his authority, Mr. Foster was a kind and generous man. He and his brilliant wife Bronja offered care and paternal guidance to all of his students during their time in Bloomington. Although he has been gone almost thirty years, his presence remains vivid, and his influence continues to affect me on a daily basis. I was so remarkably fortunate to have known Sidney Foster.

RICHARD MORRIS

I would like to pay tribute to Sidney Foster, a teacher and mentor during my graduate years at Indiana University. The years of study with Mr. Foster shaped my career, my future, my life. No other person, musically speaking, except perhaps my mother, had the influence on me that he did. For his guidance I shall always be grateful. Memories of lessons and conversations are the times I'll forever treasure.

For those of us who have pursued teaching careers, most likely we have produced students who will continue the Foster traditions. May future generations of students realize the importance of Sidney Foster, an extraordinary teacher and performer, mentor and friend.

VAL GOFF NORTON

Recollections of Sidney Foster

I first heard of Sidney Foster from a friend, Barton Frank, who had played first cello in the Vancouver British Columbia Symphony. The conductor at that time was Jacques Singer, brother of Bronja Foster. Sidney had appeared with the orchestra and my friend, the cellist, was so impressed with his performances that he talked about it for years. I happened to be one of the fortunate listeners to the praise while Barton was first cellist in the Tulsa Symphony at that time.

I had completed my Masters Degree at Tulsa University and was encouraged by Mr. Frank to apply to Indiana University to pursue a Doctor of Music in Performance degree and to study with Mr. Foster. In the meantime I was awarded a Fulbright Scholarship to Freiburg, Germany, and I completed a year there before going on to Indiana University to commence my doctoral studies in the fall of 1957.

I must say that my training with Mr. Foster was far different from any of my previous work. He embarked me upon a course of technical study to the exclusion of everything else for a period of about two months. The Vengerova approach which he had learned at Curtis Institute was of immense benefit to me and I seemed to jump to another plateau of technical achievement within a very short time.

In November of that year, I was invited to perform Bartók's Second Concerto for Piano and Orchestra in Tulsa, Oklahoma. Before my studies with Mr. Foster, I would have been unable to master the extremely technically difficult work, but with my newly found techniques I was able to master the composition within just a few months and to perform it in February.

Now I would like to speak about Mr. Foster's interpretative powers. I feel that he possessed one of the most imaginative and expressive abilities I have experienced in my entire life time. He was able to impart at least a portion of this knowledge to his students, and in my own case, my own interpretive ability expanded immeasurably. Due to his inspiration, he opened the door to my becoming a much improved pianist achieving better performances than I previously thought possible. Standing foremost in my memory is the time spent with Mr. Foster learning the Brahms Second Piano Concerto, (which I performed with Imelda Delgado so beautifully playing the orchestra part) as one of my required doctoral recitals. I shall never forget the magical moments in lesson time receiving his instructive comments as well as being totally thrilled and inspired by his own demonstration of that magnificent work.

In conclusion, I would like to state that Mr. Foster was a man of extraordinary character. Not only was he a wonderful family man, but he set an example of impeccable moral character to his students, fellow faculty, and to all that he came into contact with. I can only say that I was most blessed in being a recipient of his teaching and being favored with his warm and compassionate friendship.

WELBY PUGIN

Except for the absence of the sound of his voice and missing the enjoyment of witnessing his reaction to the response given to his latest outrageous pun or insightful witticism, it is, for me, as though Sidney were still here. Not one day has passed since August of 1966, when I first met and spoke with him outside his studio, that I haven't thought of him; and, so indelible is his imprint, that the years since December of 1976, when I last spoke with him, have done nothing to diminish his presence. Even today, as I have now attained the age that Sidney did not, I admit that he has influenced every major decision I have made: what would he say?—would he approve?—disagree?—how would he counsel? The imagined prospect of earning one of his brief and articulate rebukes—maybe even slightly more so than one of Bronja's slightly-squinched penetrating gazes—has done more to influence and shape my life than any other human factor.

The lessons he taught had remarkable relevance to the practicalities of life outside the studio and not just to the abstraction of Art that were dealt with inside the studio. The merits of thinking critically, holding uncompromising standards, delivering fair yet open-minded critiques, articulating clear defenses of opinions without being defensive or opinionated, making no-prejudicial discriminatory judgments, exhibiting grace under pressure were all manifested in the magnetic personality of this renaissance man of warmth, wit and uncommon generosity of self and spirit. Youthful immaturity, unfortunately, obscured my recognition of much of this at the time but continual reflection over the intervening years has resulted in Sidney's mentoring having extraordinarily frequent application in my personal, as well as artistic, life.

The final lesson Sidney taught me was unintentional. As I left Bloomington for the 1976 Christmas holidays, hugged him and casually wished him a Happy New Year and restful break, never did it cross my mind that that December 17 conversation would be our last. I never told Sidney how important he was to me and what my feelings were for him and the lesson he taught me was to not let these opportunities evaporate. So, responding to this lesson, I hope it's not inappropriate in this context to thank God for allowing me to share time and space with Sidney. And Bronja, Lincoln and Justin I thank you, too, for your uncommon generosity in treating us as family and sharing Sidney with us. I loved him. I love you.

JOHN REITZ

For forty-one years since I first came to know Sidney Foster in 1965, I've felt that he was the most extraordinary man I have been associated with. His quickness and fertility of mind and generosity of heart enlivened all his activities; teaching, performing, personal and collegial relationships.

After his death in 1977, Malcolm Frager wrote to Bronja, saying that even in his brief association with Sidney, he had felt that Sidney was a person who had shed more light in his 59 years than most people do in much longer life spans. I was one of a group of freshman piano students who traveled to Chicago to hear Rubinstein play the Schumann Concerto in Orchestra Hall. Sidney had asked Welby Pugin to give Rubinstein a message of greetings and regrets that he couldn't attend the concert. We went backstage and Welby relayed Sidney's message. Rubinstein grew very serious and said, "Give Mr. Foster my greetings and my deepest respect and admiration. Yes, my DEEPEST respect and admiration."

When I first played for Sidney, he said "you have learned to play the piano in a particular way, and you've gone probably as far as you can with this approach. Now we're going to learn a different way to play." I spent the next year finishing high school and playing Hanon, thrusting exercises and music in a way that sounded like Hanon. My old teacher in Portland was a little appalled at first, but I always trusted that Sidney's approach would eventually work. His aura as a teacher inspired confidence.

In lessons, Sidney never dictated to me how to play a piece. He felt that teaching in that manner too often produced puppets, not musicians. He would suggest phrase groupings, retards, pedalings, speak of metric relationships, importance of pulse, melodic shaping, relating phrases or statements to each other, balance, attention to inner lines, musicality of subordinate aspects of the music strata, overall musical architecture. His purpose was to equip students with concepts which, through the student's application, would be tools for the basis of educated and creative musicianship.

He was annoyed by careless score reading, but felt that if a musician knew the music, understood its viewpoint and purpose, he or she could do things differently than the composer indicated in his editorial role. But this should be the result of thought and experimentation. Sidney appreciated instinctive musicality, but felt that the artist is an educated musician. When Horowitz came to Bloomington to play a recital, Sidney spoke to the Sunday performance class, saying that he didn't know how well Horowitz would play, but he did know that Horowitz's preparation would have been completely thorough. Every note would have been thought about in its musical function.

Sidney was not an advocate of the "definitive" performance. He felt that the artist should be able to play every piece and every passage in different ways, so that the music-making process can be a flexible time art rather than a process of attempting to recreate the ultimate musical sculpture over and over, like a recording.

Once at a party Sidney gave for his students, a rather combative student once said to Sidney, "Some people feel that you have a messianic complex in your teaching." Sidney thought for a moment, then responded, "That is true to the extent that, to be effective, any teacher must believe that what they have to teach is valid and necessary, and must believe that they are able or 'chosen' to teach it."

Before one of Sidney's faculty recitals, the Daily Student published an interview with him. The interviewer had commented that some people feel that the piano had become a museum piece, with its aging repertoire and long tradition of formal recitals. Sidney's response was "For those who think that, welcome to my museum!"

While not always admiring Rubinstein's playing, Sidney always admired his approach to performance, which treated performance as a celebration rather than an ordeal. When I came here to Kenyon, I met a drama teacher here who knew Sidney's faculty recitals at Indiana because they had often coincided with theater openings which Harlene traveled to Bloomington to attend. She remembered fondly that "His playing had such a joy of life."

We can all be thankful for so much of Sidney's life that he shared with us.

ALBERTO REYES

Sidney Foster's Legacy

Sidney Foster was the ideal teacher. His articulate insight about the means of his art enabled him to transmit with eloquence and precision the accumulated knowledge of a lifetime of thinking about music. His sympathetic awareness of the minefield that is the psychological relationship between artist and pupil made the process of studying with him an opportunity for emotional growth as well as musical development.

His generosity with his time and resources was legendary. He thought nothing of welcoming into his home and family a young pianist from abroad whose parents didn't have the means of financing his education in this country. He would listen until well past midnight at Indiana University's Recital Hall to the program of a student preparing for the Tchaikovsky Competition or for his or hers first junior recital; or of entertaining lavishly and frequently his entire class . . . all this with unvarying good cheer, wit, charm, and intellectual acuity.

He seemed satisfied with a few public appearances a year, and New York heard him regularly at Carnegie Hall, Alice Tully Hall, and Lincoln Center. But he didn't hanker for the life of the touring virtuoso, nor did he pursue a recording career.

Sidney Foster's art lives in the treasured memories of his listeners and in the tapes of some of his live concert appearances.

PATSY HODGES SEYBERT

Do you remember the aroma of pipe tobacco when Sidney was in the Music Building?

He could not stand fingernails that clicked on the keys. Dallas Weekley was escorted to Brummett's Drug Store by Sidney to purchase clippers!

When I boasted of having "perfect pitch," Sidney laid his entire left arm on the keys!

When the Fosters moved from their apartment to a house, all his students pitched in to help wherever needed. I had a closet to paint—dark brown! I never did figure that out!

A substitute teacher filled in for Sidney while he was on tour who told us: don't wash dishes; it will ruin your hands. Don't lift heavy suitcases, it will hurt the muscles in your hands. Sidney simply scoffed. He told us washing was good for your fingers, and lifting a suitcase made you stronger.

Once, while I was in a lesson, Sidney stopped me and said, "Listen." Outside his window was a cardinal, either trying to outdo me or to sing along. We never knew which!

How guilty I feel writing this when I know Sidney must have been so disappointed when I dropped my music and married. All his time gone, wasted.

I am not a concert pianist, nor a teacher, but Sidney taught me how to work to my ability, patience, and respect. My music has been in my life. I just found out that my girls would dance in the hall outside their rooms when I would practice at night.

Thank you, dear Sidney. And, Bronja, thank you for sharing Sidney with all his students and being there for him. You have been like my second family always.

ROBERT C. SMITH

In the fall of 1960 I was beginning my fifth season of what had proven to be a fairly successful New York based performing and teaching career. Dame Fortune had dealt kindly with me but inherently I knew that this was not how or where I wanted to spend the remainder of my career. My undergraduate studies had been as part of a municipal environment at the Philadelphia Conservatory of Music, but somehow I felt the lack of campus life and the concomitant academic energy and stimulus. Academia had always exerted a strong tug and at this point in my development, I decided that perhaps advanced graduate study was the route to investigate.

One of my hometown musical associates was a violinist and theorist named Howard Boatwright who, at the time, was teaching as Hindemith's assistant at Yale. As fate or luck would have it, we were both at home in Virginia for Christmas and our paths crossed at a dinner party. Yale seemed a viable option and I asked what my chances might be for obtaining a graduate assistantship there. "Why do you want that?" He asked in reply to my question. I told him that I had decided to pursue a university future. Without a moment's hesitation he replied, "If that is your intention, there's only one place for you. Go to Indiana University and get a doctorate in performance." At the time, Indiana University was just beginning to cause ripples that would later result in its musical tidal waves and therefore while I was aware of its name, I wasn't (in my east coast ivory tower) intimately acquainted with its consequences.

Upon return to New York, I called another friend, Harvey Wedeen, a pianist and native New Yorker who was widely connected musically and socially. I apprised him of my intentions and of Howard's advice and asked if he knew anything about the Indiana University Jacobs School of Music. "Just a bit," he replied, "but some good friends of ours are in town for the end of semester vacation and could tell you anything you want to know. Why don't you come for lunch tomorrow and meet them?"

And thus I met Sidney and Bronja for the first time. Lunch was the usual warm and witty exchange that was always manifest in their company. I told Sidney of my interest in pursuing the doctorate. He was strongly supportive and inquired as to my immediate plans. I informed him that I was leaving at the end of that week to embark on a nine-week Community Concert tour with a vocal trio and would find it difficult to do very much formal applying at that juncture. He suggested that I write a letter of intent to Dean Bain apprising him of my musical background and experience and he, in turn, would go back to Bloomington, talk to the Dean and "see what he could do."

Somewhere on tour in small-town America, I received a letter from Dean Bain. It informed me that pending acceptance of my graduate entrance recital and the successful surmounting of the graduate placement hurdles, I would be a candidate in the doctoral performance program. I was also offered what was, in those days, a very generous assistantship. And so a new path opened ahead.

Arrival that fall on the stupendous Bloomington campus is still a vivid memory quite easily recalled today. The excitement of finally being a part of a university, heretofore an unknown component of my musical education, was heady, indeed.

An invitation to dinner at South Jordan was immediately forthcoming, the first of many that were to ensue. Here the warmth and benevolence that were so abundant Chez Foster unfolded. The term "Instant Friendship Available Here" could easily have been emblazoned over their door. The welcome mat never disappeared, no matter what the hour. A tuna sandwich at midnight was readily available from Bronja's kitchen.

My first session in the studio came next. Up until now, Sidney had not heard me play. I presented a sampling from my imminent entrance recital and he listened intently and sympathetically and without interruption. When I had concluded he said, in that marvelously direct and slightly staccato manner of his, "Young man, you play the piano in spite of yourself." I was well aware of this but couldn't discern the reason. My musical tutelage had been regarded as fairly high caliber and with some distinguished names but I had never been taught anything about the mechanics of playing, the subtleties of tone production or how to listen. My practicing was confined to "do it over; faster or slower, louder or softer." As he said in our first lesson, after I had successfully negotiated the mine field of doctoral entrance audition and placement exams and been officially accepted into the studio, "You are able to run but you never learned to walk. Would you be willing to backtrack a bit and acquire a few basics?"

Three years in residence enabled me to complete the course work and make inroads into the eight required recitals. And what those three years produced! Being a part of the Foster studio not only resulted in a musical, technical dimension that I had sought unsuccessfully up until now, it also provided a collegial warmth and supportive ambience that resonate within me to this day. Not only the musical stimulus of the lessons, but the reassurance of being the last lesson of the day, Sidney would say, "Let's go see what Bronja has for dinner." The deferential respect that existed in the studio was somehow transplanted to an almost familial acceptance at the dining table.

And accompanying all of those occasions was that indelible part of Sidney's personality that those of us privileged to know him can never forget—his sense of humor: omnipresent, deft and immediately ready in a riposte. It seems apt to recall one of my first observations of it. All who knew them were aware that the Fosters were acknowledged nocturnal mammals. The first week of the fall semester five of us met in the studio to establish a mutually agreed upon time to hold the Romantic seminar. After several unsuccessful proposals a younger member of the doctoral brigade proffered eagerly, "What about Tuesday or Thursday at 8:00 a.m.?" With alacrity Sidney countered, "8:00 a.m.! Don't be absurd, young man, I couldn't possibly stay up that late."

EVA M. VOUKLIZAS

My first encounter with Mr. Sidney Foster occurred many years before my period of study with him. I do not recall how I came to be at Lincoln Auditorium in Syracuse, New York attending a performance of the Minneapolis Symphony conducted by Dimitri Mitropoulos. I do remember sitting in the balcony completely fascinated by the bald head of the conductor which glistened under the many lights in that enormous hall. At one point during the concert, I was very surprised to see a slender man walk onto the stage. He sat down at the piano that had been moved from the back to the front of the stage. In retrospect, I find it very interesting that I do not remember any of the works the orchestra played but I do recall his playing the Brahms Concerto in B flat. I also remember loving the work so much that I wished I were talented enough to play it. To this very day, it still remains a favorite.

My next contact with Mr. Foster was on the campus of Indiana University. I was studying with Mr. Frederick Baldwin at that time and when I walked on stage to begin my Master's program, I was shocked to see Mr. Foster walking down the aisle to find a seat. I remember being so surprised that he came to hear me play. Seeing him increased the degree of my nervousness. For the most part, I had observed that piano faculty members hardly ever attended the student recitals of other piano professors. They were obligated to attend the hearings but not the recitals.

A few weeks after my recital, I decided to stay on for additional work, and I decided to change teachers. Because he was always kind to me and came to my recital, I felt comfortable in asking Mr. Foster if he would consider teaching me. The following is an example of the man's loyalty to his friends. To quote Mr. Foster: "Fred Baldwin is my closest friend on this faculty and I do not want him to be hurt. You have to do this yourself. You have to talk to him. Otherwise, I will not teach you." I did eventually study with Mr. Foster and signed up for his Romantic music seminar as an elective. He canceled class one day in order to drive up to the Indianapolis airport to pick up Arthur Rubinstein who was to play a recital in Fisher Auditorium. Several of us in the class, including Foster students, patiently waited near the elevators on the second floor, hoping that the two men would come our way. They finally stepped from the elevator and Mr. Foster looked at us, totally ignored us and guided Mr. Rubinstein to show him the practice rooms on the second floor of the circular building. When they returned to the elevators, he grinned at us and then said, "I would like you to meet some of the students." I audaciously walked a few steps toward Mr. Rubinstein, looked at his twinkling blue eyes and thought, "I am almost as tall as he is." I asked him how he liked the new building. He responded that he liked it very much, and did we know that the Paris Conservatory had bars on the windows and resembled a prison.

As I reflect on my study with Mr. Foster, I realize that he was always articulate and direct in what he said. I was playing the slow introduction of the Mendelssohn *Rondo Capriccioso* when he stopped me and said "You are a talented lady but a musical slob." I was hurt, but many months later, I realized what he was trying to teach me. He was not saying to control your emotions when you play, but rather to plan how you execute the phrases for the ultimate goal of expressive playing.

CHARLES H. WEBB

It is a great pleasure to write this letter of appreciation for my classes and lessons with Professor Sidney Foster. Although he was not my primary teacher of piano, it was my privilege to study and perform my final doctoral recital under his tutelage. My regular teacher, Professor Walter Robert, was on sabbatical leave, and I asked Professor Foster if I could work with him on my final recital. Thankfully he said yes, and so I had the great fortune of spending an entire semester in his studio.

This was not my first study with Sidney, however. During my initial semester as a doctoral student in the fall of 1958, I enrolled in Sidney's doctoral seminar, which covered the Romantic Period of piano music. I remember how amazed the entire class was at his encyclopedic knowledge of the vast body of nineteenth-century piano literature and his ability to demonstrate from memory many of the gigantic works composed during that era. He skillfully guided the class as we studied analysis, form, performance practice—indeed all the elements of many of the most significant works of that time. Sidney kept the discussions on target and demanded that each student lead the discussion of a particular work and then demonstrate it by a performance in class. I remember his showing us his "human side" one day when a student asked him how to spell "Faschingsschwank aus Wien"—that rambling and difficult work of Robert Schumann. He replied after trying it several ways, "I don't know how to spell that. I just play it!"

It was the private lessons with Sidney Foster, however, that inspired me most. He performed often in public, and I remember marveling at the beautiful melodic lines that he could make and the infinite gradations of sound his impeccable touch produced. To have an opportunity to learn first-hand how he did this and to develop an overall sense of style and scope of the Brahms F minor Piano Sonata and the Prokofiev Fourth Sonata will remain with me always. Yes, he was demanding, but always with some humor and with the feeling that he was always supporting you. Perhaps the most telling aspect of his teaching is the fact that even today, over forty years after studying that semester with Sidney, I think of what I learned from him every time I sit at the piano. His insight, intellect, common sense, and overwhelming desire to see his students succeed, all contributed to make him a truly great teacher.

WEEKLEY AND ARGANBRIGHT, PIANO-DUETTISTS

I, Dallas, began my study with Mr. Foster in 1953 at Indiana University. At that time the Fosters were living in "University Apartments," where I was invited along with other students to dinner, and I felt honored to be included. I had been brought up in the Florida Everglades and knew so little about the world; I was the first in my family to see snow! Clearly I had a lot to learn, both musically and in nearly every aspect of life.

Mr. Foster was very kind and patient with me. I was once playing *L'isle Joyeuse* and he looked at me sternly during a section of three-against-five and said "I will not tell you again to correct this rhythm by next week!" So I went up and down the halls playing it for everyone who would listen, for assurance that it was "right." At my next lesson I began to play, and when I came to this section he began to tap on a table. In a panic, I tried to coordinate my playing with this tapping, but my performance was falling to pieces. I said in frustration "I'm sorry Mr. Foster, but I can't follow that beat." He replied "I'm only cleaning my pipe!"

Another anecdote: once when Mr. Foster was demonstrating a passage for me I was standing beside him, unaware that the side of my hip was silently holding down a few of the lowest bass notes. When he came to the end of the section, which he played with exceptional beauty, he said "That's you" (meaning that I was causing those bass notes to continue ringing) and I replied "Oh! Thank you!"

I completed my B.M. in 1955 and my M.M. in 1957, at which time Nancy Arganbright and I were married (53 years ago!). Nancy had studied with Mr. Foster for a semester while Walter Robert was on a sabbatical leave. When I began my doctoral work at Indiana University in 1960, Dean Bain was very kind in permitting us to tailor my degree to emphasize piano duets, since we had just gone under N.Y. management in that same year. Mr. Foster coached us tirelessly in preparation for our Carnegie Hall recital debut in 1963. After spending 1964 in Vienna, establishing our career in Europe and gathering research for my doctoral dissertation on Schubert's piano duets, Mr. Foster suggested that we transfer our study to Mr. Robert, since he was Viennese and exceptionally interested in the Viennese classicists, my proposed subject matter and performance emphasis.

Mr. Foster was such a great influence on Nancy and me that his spirit has continued to sit on our shoulders as we practice and perform, still hoping to bring a smile of approval to his face.

I, Nancy, was a solo pianist with Mr. Foster for only one semester, since he then suffered a heart attack. However, his emphasis at that time was on my technique, and he scheduled several shorter lessons per week to that end. I have always given Mr. Foster total credit for my technical development. Through 40 years of concert touring and teaching, I have never once experienced any physical strain or injury in my hands, to the point that I am amazed to see the amount of attention which is being paid to such strain/injuries nowadays. I am grateful to Mr. Foster for making my hands capable of expressing what I wanted to say through the great composers, and for sparing me any physical problems or discomfort in these hands. His memory continues to be an inspiration to both of us.

PAUL WIRTH

Sidney Foster did not leave behind a very large number of piano recordings. This is unfortunate because I'm sure the world would have enjoyed and even been ennobled by them. Nor did he write any books on piano technique. This, too, is a loss because they would have been indispensable.

What he did leave, mainly, was "Sidney Foster students." The people he taught still carry around the part of him that they were fortunate enough to experience and understand. The example he set and the power of his ideas live on in his students, continuously transforming them and creating familiar but unexpected little miracles.

This may be, ironically, an even better legacy than any recordings or books that are "frozen in time." Sidney Foster left a living, creative, and re-creative presence in his students, one that continues to evolve from the purity of the principles he lived and taught.

I can think of no greater legacy.

VEDA ZUPONCIC

Memories of Sidney Foster

I can't say why I chose Indiana University as a possible music school for myself while I was a high school student. I can't say for sure why I chose either Sidney Foster or Abbey Simon as possible teachers. We didn't have the Internet, and except for the brief listing of academic credentials on the faculty list in the catalogue, there was precious little information to help a 16-year-old girl from a remote northern Minnesota town make a momentous decision about the person who would be the most important figure in her personal and professional life.

The summer of my junior year of high school, I found the least expensive music camp in the upper Midwest: Northern Illinois University. While there, I studied with Dr. Robert Floyd, a superb and caring teacher; he asked me about my plans for college. I told him I wanted to study at Indiana, and, as a student of Sidney Foster, he immediately began to sing Mr. Foster's praises and I never looked back.

A few months later, Mr. Foster was scheduled to play a recital in Duluth, Minnesota. The night of the concert, a blizzard of considerable proportions—even for northern Minnesota—blew into town. Duluth was 60 miles south from my hometown; our car was loaded with sand, blankets and a shovel and it took my father more than two hours to get me to the concert. Perhaps 50 people were in the audience and as the diminutive Mr. Foster walked on the stage to take his seat at the piano, my father, ever the gentle punster said, "He really has an ear for music.'

The program included the Rachmaninoff Second Sonata. As Mr. Foster finished the second movement, he stopped, turned to the audience and said, "It appears something is wrong with the pedal. Let me see if I can correct the problem." He got down on all fours under the piano, re-engaged the rod that operated the pedal, to the great amusement of the audience, and got back on the bench to finish the sonata with huge effect.

I was too young, too unconscious to have had the presence of mind to keep a diary about Mr. Foster's many witticisms and turns of phrase. But I treasure the scores in which he marked such basic—basically brilliant, that is—indications about phrasing, architecture and pedaling. I can trace my first real, professional comprehension of musical form by his markings in my copy of the Mendelssohn *Fantasy in F Sharp minor*, the first piece of big repertoire assigned following the technical regime we all enjoyed.

The technical approach was easy for me and I relished bouncing around the keyboard and making lots of sound. It took me many years to understand that this was just a tiny corner of what Mr. Foster had to offer as a professor. Too often, students' memories of playing Hanon exercises subsume memories of the great artistic lessons taught. Learning how to listen, how to create a musical conversation, to illuminate the form for the audience, were really his greatest gifts to me. Increasingly, I value his taste: Sit still and play with clarity and from your heart. He taught us how to play with imagination, yet with honesty: Honest fingers, honest emotion and honest intelligence. Everything important that I needed as a pianist I received in large measure from Mr. Foster. His genius in choosing repertoire for his student was transformational. How could he see that big Romantic works were my ticket, my meat? He knew me much better than I knew myself, most certainly.

In my first semester at Indiana University, Mr. Foster made his momentous tour of the Soviet Union. I still have a copy of the newspaper clipping with the picture of Mr. Foster in front of the poster bearing his name in large Cyrillic letters. There he stood, wearing a Russian shapka with a big smile on his face. Upon his return, he presented all the ladies in the studio with little bottles of Russian perfume. I kept mine for many, many years. I can still recall the scent—it really was something lovely.

After living through the increasingly rough-and-tumble life in 20th and 21st century academia, I can only marvel at the gentlemanly professor with whom I had the good fortune to study. He had the highest expectations, the greatest vocabulary, and the loftiest personal conduct. Can you imagine: There I sat, a simple 17-year-old girl dressed in cutoffs and a Madras shirt, when Abbey Simon walked into the studio. Mr. Foster introduced me, "Mr. Simon, let me introduce Miss Zuponcic." I was treated like a great lady and I have never forgotten the incident.

I recall being in Mrs. Irving Fell's home for a party after my masters recital in 1968. Jorge Bolet had just joined the faculty and Mr. Foster, Mr. Simon, and Mr. Bolet sat near me, trying to decide with whom I should study when I moved east. Their communal decision was Ilona Kabos. I might be one of the few who studied for some length with another teacher, and then had the opportunity to return to play for Mr. Foster. I brought another set of ears and the experience that simply comes with years when I played for him in the early 70's. Every lesson was a gift—literally and figuratively, since he refused to accept a fee. I had already studied *Venezia i Napoli* with Mme. Kabos, but Mr. Foster provided me with phenomenal fingerings, concepts about style and fresh ideas that were eagerly received. This time around, I was paying attention! I have so valued having had only two important teachers in my adult life. In these days, students seem to want a smorgasbord of technical and artistic approaches, to the point that they are almost self-taught. It takes time—and sometimes distance of time—to drink from the source. I am Mr. Foster's product and I bear—imperfectly—the stamp of that artist's ideas. I can legitimately pass on some of what I learned to another generation, knowing from whence it came and its proven value in my lifetime of playing the piano.

I intruded upon Mr. Foster and his family one last time before his surgery in Boston. I was so grateful to be able to say good-bye to him, and to tell him how much he meant to me, that I loved him. I told him, "Mr. Foster, you must get well and write a book." He said, "Veda, you must write it." "But Mr. Foster, I understand only some of what you know. I know how to put my weight on the keyboard to make big sound. How do you play softly?" "Well, you just take the weight away." There it was, in his last days, his last basically brilliant advice to me.

A few days later, there was a last minute cancellation at SUNY New Paltz, and I substituted for the indisposed pianist. As I feverishly worked to prepare the recital, we received word of Mr. Foster's passing. I wept as I was driven to New Paltz, played as well as I could under the circumstances, and remember saying to the audience before playing an encore, "It would be presumptuous of me to dedicate this Scriabin Etude to the memory of my great teacher, Sidney Foster, who passed away yesterday. It was a work he played incomparably but I will do my best t o do it justice." I have been fortunate to have sat at the foot of a genius and have always regretted that I couldn't have risen further to fulfill the promise he found in me.

I can never repay the many kindnesses he showed me. I can only try to do the same for my students.

Appendix C

Cadenza to the Beethoven *Piano Concerto No. 3 in C Minor,* OP. 37, 1941

Cadenza to the Beethoven Piano Concerto #3 in C Minor

(As played by Sidney Foster with the New York Philharmonic)

By Sidney Foster

Figure C.1.1. Cadenza by Sidney Foster. Copyright Bronja S. Foster, all rights reserved.

Appendix C

Figure C.1.2. Cadenza by Sidney Foster. Copyright Bronja S. Foster, all rights reserved.

Cadenza *to the Beethoven* Piano Concerto No. 3 in C Minor, OP. 37, *1941*

Figure C.1.3. Cadenza by Sidney Foster. Copyright Bronja S. Foster, all rights reserved.

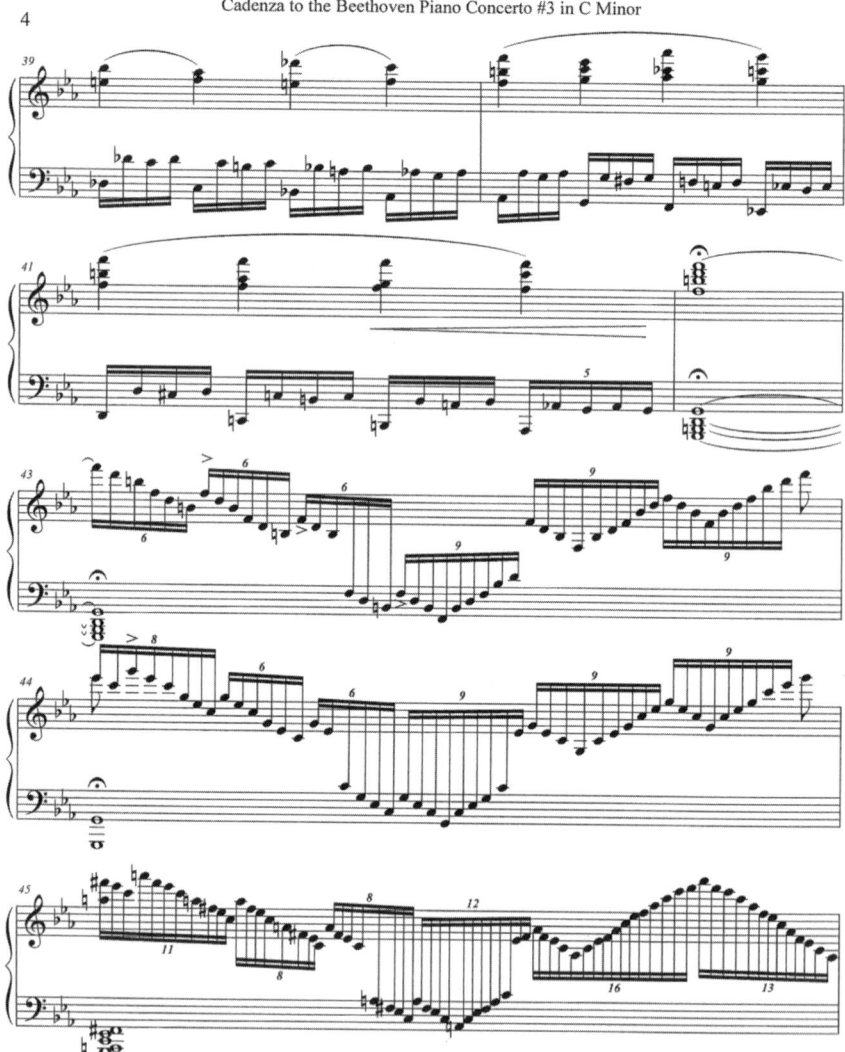

Figure C.1.4. Cadenza by **Sidney Foster**. Copyright Bronja S. Foster, all rights reserved.

Cadenza *to the Beethoven* Piano Concerto No. 3 in C Minor, OP. 37, *1941*

Figure C.1.5. Cadenza by Sidney Foster. Copyright Bronja S. Foster, all rights reserved.

Index

Abbott Kirk, Jane, 120, 122
Abosch, David (born in 1928) and Irene R. (born in 1935), xiii, 88-89
Abram, Jacques, 5, 70-71
Abravanel, Maurice (1903–1993), 35
Alice Tully Hall, 25, 29, 31-32, 49, 159
Allison, Irl (1896–1979), 52
American Society of Ancient Instruments, 74
Antoine's Restaurant, 89
Apel, Willi (1893–1988), 61, 63, 145

Bach, Johann Sebastian (1685–1750), 9, 19-20, 27, 30-31, 60-61, 63, 117
Bain, Wilfred C., 48, 62, 135
Baldwin, Fred, 35, 163
Ball, Alan, 102
Barber, Samuel (1910–1981), 72
Barbirolli, Sir John (1899–1970), 14, 34
Bartok, Bela (1881–1945), vi, 31, 43, 85, 90, 96, 98, 156
Battista, Joseph and Mrs., 49, 105
Beethoven, Ludwig van (1770–1827), vii, 9, 14, 19-21, 27, 31-32, 34, 57-58, 70, 90, 94, 103, 111, 116-17, 129-30, 142-43, 148, 170-76
Berkshire Quartet, 58
Berne, Mary, 5

Berner, Rosalie Leventritt (died in 1983), 13
Berner, T. Roland (1910-1990), 13
Bernstein, Leonard (1918–1990), 12, 72, 90
Boepple, Hans, 120, 124
Boieldieu, François (1775–1834), 17
The Bohemians, 13
Bolet, Jorge (1914–1990), xi, 5, 12, 24, 48, 50, 64, 123, 145, 168
Boston Globe, 98
Boston Hospital, 21, 105-6
Boston Symphony Orchestra, 35, 43, 96
Boston University School for the Fine and Applied Arts, 21
Brady, Patricia, 120, 126
Brahms, Johannes (1833–1897), 12, 14, 27, 30, 34, 75, 98, 116, 125, 156, 163-64
Brandes, Lew, 120, 128
Bronstein, Rafael, 69
Brown County State Park, 77, 134
Busch, Adolf (1891–1952), 14

Carnegie A440 Pizza Hall, 79
Carnegie Hall, ix, xiii, 6-7, 13-14, 19-23, 28-34, 49, 57, 60, 90, 93-94, 104-5, 143, 159, 165
Chicago Symphony Orchestra, 35

Index

Chopin, Frédéric (1810–1849), 4,19-20, 27-29, 31-32, 43, 52, 55-56, 81, 87-88, 93, 103, 133-35, 140, 151
Clementi, Muzio (1752–1832) *Sonatinas,* 104
Cliburn, Van, 49, 106, 122
Cohen, Mrs., 5
Coleman, Harry, 107
Colorado State Penitentiary, Cañon, Colorado, 6
Colorado Symphony Orchestra, 88
Concert Hall–Minsk, Russia, 91
Concerto Highlights and company, vi, 85, 88-89, 91
Conservatory Great Hall–Moscow, Russia, 91
Copland, Aaron (1900–1990), 35, 43, 85, 93, 96, 98
Covent Garden in London, 35
Curtis Institute of Music, ix, xi, xiii, 5, 8, 23, 35, 74
Czerny, Carl (1791–1857), 52, 129, 134, 140, 144, 154

Dallas Symphony Orchestra, 35, 48, 62, 75
Damrosch, Walter (1862–1950), 25, 33-34, 36, 70
Danin, Victoria, 74
Davis, Agnes, 58
Debussy, Claude (1862–1918), 19, 28
Delgado, Imelda, v, ix, xii, 120-21, 133, 156
Dello Joio, Norman (1913–2008), v, xiv, 1, 9, 16-22, 34
Del Mar College, 23, 94, 101-2, 120
Diamond, Anna (Foster). *See* Foster, Anna Diamond (mother of Sidney)
DiFazio, Dorothy (Dottie) Foster, xiv, 4, 65, 68
DiFazio, Louis, 69, 88
Dohnanyi, Ernst von (1877–1960), 17, 28, 31-32
Dorati, Antal (1906–1988), 35-36

Doty, E(zra) William (1907–1994), 51
Drummond, Miss, 5, 8-9

Effron, David, 120, 136
Elman, Mischa (1891–1967), 57-58
Essipova, Annette (1851–1914), 42, 72
Eto, Toshiya 59

Finkelstein, Louis, 3, 35. *See also* Foster, Louis (Finkelstein) (father of Sidney)
Firkusny, Rudolf (1912–1994), 101
Fleisher, Leon, 101, 146
Flier, Yakov (1912–1977), vi, 85, 90, 93-94
Florida State University, x, 47, 52-53, 128, 137
Floyd, Carlisle, 52-53, 120, 137
Floyd, JB, xiii, 120, 122, 138
Fokine, Michel (1880–1942), 25, 35-36
Foster, Anna Diamond (mother of Sidney), vi, 3, 65, 68
Foster, Bronja Singer (wife of Sidney), xiv, 10, 12, 14, 33, 51, 54, 65, 74-78, 91-92, 94, 105-6, 128-62
Foster, Justin, (son of Sidney), xiv, 78, 84, 93, 104, 129, 137, 139, 142, 150, 157
Foster, Lincoln, (son of Sidney), xiv, 106, 139, 142, 150, 157
Foster (Finkelstein), Louis (father of Sidney), vi, 3-4, 8, 67-68, 85, 87, 104
Franck, César (1822–1890), 28, 32, 117
Frank, Barton, 155
Frank, Claude, 101
Frantz, Dalies (1908–1965), 51
Froschauer, Helmuth (born 1933), 35
Freire, Helena, 120, 139

Gargarian, Miriam, 120, 140
Gershwin, George (1898–1937), 88
Gilels, Emil (1916–1985), 32, 93-94
Gingold, Josef (1909–1995), 58, 145
Godowsky, Leopold (1870–1938), 41, 45

Goldstein, Walter (1923–2008), 46
Golub, Herbert and Ina, 120, 141
Goode, Richard (born in 1943), 101
Gordon, Nat, 37
Gould, Morton (1913–1996), 88
Gould, Walter A. (died in 2007), 88
Gradova, Gitta (1904–1985), 101
Graffman, Gary (born in 1928), 72, 101
Greenhouse, Bernard (born in 1916), 53
Grieg, Edvard (1843–1907), 36, 88, 133, 138

Hamilton, Robert, 121, 143
Hanon, Charles-Louis (1819–1900), 52, 109, 129, 134, 140, 142, 153-54, 158, 167
Hargail Music Press, 20
Harrison, Eric, 35
Herbert Barrett Management, 59
Hersh, Alan, 121, 147
Hilsberg, Alexander, 69
Hofmann, Josef (1876–1957), ix, xi, 5, 8, 32, 41-42, 73
Horowitz, Vladimir (1903–1989), 32, 93, 146, 158
Horszowski, Mieczysław (1892–1993), 101
Hurok, Sol (1888–1974), 35-36

Indianapolis Symphony Orchestra, xii, 35, 37, 69, 78, 132, 152, 154
Indiana University, 20-21, 36, 39, 42-43, 48-50, 57, 61-64, 68, 77, 79, 82, 90-91, 93, 106, 113, 120, 123-29, 132-33, 136-37, 139
International Musician, 53

Jacobs School of Music, Indiana University, ix, x, xiii, 122, 161
Jewish Advocate, 98
John, 67
Johnson, President Lyndon B. (1908–1973), 91
Jones, Mason, 75

Judson, Arthur, 14
Juilliard School of Music, xiv, 6

Kaizer, Edward, 121, 148
Kaplan, Sol, 12, 75, 94
Karr, Gary, 53
Kay, Hershey, 12
Kennedy, President John F., 91
Knopow, Mini, 77
Korn, Richard, 23, 36

Leinsdorf, Erich, 96, 98
LeRoy, René, 9, 16-18, 20, 58
Leventritt, Justice David (Supreme Court), 12
Leventritt, Edgar M., 12-13, 15, 102
Leventritt Foundation, 13, 102
Leventritt Competition, ix, 6, 12-14, 16, 23, 34, 47, 51, 75, 102, 151
Leventritt, Rosalie M. (daughter), ix, 13
Lewisohn Stadium 23, 36
Lhevinne, Joseph and Rosina ix, 41
Lincoln Center for the Performing Arts, 25, 29, 49, 159
Lin, Chiu-Ling, 121, 150
Liszt, Franz (1811–1886), 31-32, 63, 94, 121, 135, 152-53

MacDowell Club and Competition, 12, 23, 27, 34, 47, 51, 102
MacWatters, Virginia, 75
Mana-Zucca Cassel (1891–1981), vi, 65, 70, 72
Martinů, Bohuslav (1890–1959), 9, 16, 18
Masselos, William (1920–1992), 101
Mastroianni, Thomas, 121, 152
Matthews, Caryl, 121, 152
Matthews, Joseph, 121, 154
Mendelssohn, Felix (1809–1847), 30, 43, 164, 167
Metropolitan Opera House, 23, 36
Miami Conservatory, 5
Miller, Frank, 87
Miller, W. F., 5

Minneapolis Symphony Orchestra, 34, 87, 163
Mitropoulos, Dimitri (1896–1960), 34-37, 78, 163
Molkin, Winfred, 46
Montecino, Alfonso, 49, 82
Morris, Richard, 121, 154-55
Mozart, Wolfgang Amadeus (1756–1791), 21, 30, 32, 43, 92, 104, 117, 125
Musical America, ix, 31
Music Educator Round Table, 63
Musical Heritage Society, Inc., 104-5
Music Journal, 63

NBC Orchestra, 69
National Concert Artists' Corporation, 34, 57
National Guild of Piano Teachers, 52
National Orchestral Association, 23
New England Medical Center, 105
New Orleans Morning Tribune, 46
New Orleans Philharmonic, 69
Newcomb School of Music, 46
Newstead, Arthur (1881–1952), 46
New York Philharmonic, ix, xiii, 9, 14, 16, 23, 34, 36, 70, 88, 90, 101, 104
New York Post, 31
New York Sun, 25
New York Times, 30
North Texas State University, 48, 62-63
Norton, Val Goff, 122, 155
The Notation of Polyphonic Music, 61

Oppenheimer, Amy and Harry, 12
Ovation to Sidney Foster, 2 CD set, IPAM 1204, 60; 45

Patty Foot, 84
Piano Guild of Texas, 52
PM Daily, 15
Potomac Watergate Amphitheatre, 23
Pressler, Menachem (born in 1923), 64
Program Concert in Russia, 168
Program Poster–Russian, 95

Pulitzer Prize, 21
Pugin, Welby, 122, 157

Rachmaninoff, Sergei (1873-1943), ix, xii, 25, 30, 35-36, 41, 43, 90, 93-94, 120, 125, 142, 146, 167
Radio City Music Hall Orchestra, 35, 69
Rapée, Erno, 35
Reisenberg, Nadia, 14, 101
Reitz, John, 122, 157
Revueltas, Silvestre (1899–1940), 10
Reyes, Alberto, 93, 109, 122, 159
Richter, Sviatoslav, 93-94
Robert, Walter, 11, 58, 63, 106, 164-65
Roosevelt Hotel, 87
Rose, Leonard (1918–1984), 57, 75-77
Rubinstein, Anton (1829–1894), 41
Rubinstein, Arthur (1887–1982), 163
Rudolf, Max (1902–1995), 101

Salmond, Felix (1888–1952), 57
Sam's Subway, 78
Saperton, David (1889-1970), 5, 27-28, 41-42, 48, 73, 75, 87, 143, 152
Scalero, Rosario (1870–1954), 9
Schelling, Ernest (1876–1939), xii, 36-37, 102, 106-7, 130-33
Scholz, János (1903–1993), v, 1, 9, 11-12
Schonberg, Harold C. (1915–2003), 90
Schumann, Robert (1810–1856), 28, 30-31, 43, 90, 117-18, 130, 142, 148
Scriabin, Alexander (1872–1915), 31-32, 41, 169
Serkin, Rudolf (1903–1991), 14, 101
Sevitsky, Fabián (1900–1988), 69
Seybert, Patsy Hodges, 122, 160
Shakespeare (1564–1616), 5
Shenandoah Elementary School, 5
Shenk, M. N., 30
Silvera, Señor E., 9-11
Simon, Abbey (born in 1922), xi, xiv, 12, 48-50, 64, 123, 145, 154, 167-68
Simon, Henry, 15

Singer, Jacques (brother of Mrs.Bronja Singer Foster), 14, 35, 74-75, 133, 138, 156
Smith, Earl Chester, 5, 8, 46, 70
Smith, Robert C., 122, 160
Solomon, Izler (1910–1987) 35
The Stad Family, 74
Steinberg, William (1899–1978), 35, 101
Steinway Company, 101-2
Steinway Hall, 13
Stern, Isaac (1920–2001) and Solomon, 41, 57
St. Petersburg Times (Florida), 30
Sunday Herald, 98

Tass News, Moscow, Russia, 93
Towne, Ted, 81
Thomson, Virgil (1896–1989), 10
Toscanini, Arturo (1867–1957), 69
Town Hall, New York City, 9, 11, 16-17, 20, 23, 27-28, 57, 102, 138
Tchaikovsky Great Hall in Moscow, 91

Uninsky, Alexander (1910–1972), 78-79
University of California, San Diego, 79

University of Florida, Tallahassee, 120
University of Miami Conservatory, 5
University of Texas, Austin, 51
University of Vermont, 5, 93
Utah Symphony Orchestra, 35

Vardi, Emmanuel (born in 1915), 69
Vengerova, Isabel (1877–1956), vi, 5, 42, 46-47, 65, 72-73, 143, 156
Vienna Chamber Orchestra, 35, 104
Viggie, 82-83
Vosary, Ms., 8-9
Vouklizas, Eva M., 122, 163

The War of the Worlds, 76
Watson, Jack M., 63
Webb, Dean Charles H., v, x, xiii, 106, 122, 164
Weber, Carl Maria von (1786–1826), 18, 154
Weekley, Dallas and Nancy, 78, 122, 160, 165
Wilde, Oscar (1854–1900), 75
Wirth, Paul, 77, 122, 166

Zuponcic, Veda, 122, 166, 168

About the Author

Imelda Delgado.

As a scholarship student at Indiana University, **Imelda Delgado** earned the performance Master's and Doctoral degrees studying piano with Sidney Foster. She received the coveted Performer's Certificate for her Master's piano recital and was awarded a two-year Ford Foundation grant to complete her doctoral studies.

Her solo and chamber music performances have been in the United States, England, Mexico, Switzerland, and Italy. She has held teaching positions at Del Mar College, Corpus Christi State University (currently Texas A&M University in Corpus Christi) in Texas, the University of Vermont in Burlington, and at Stephens College in Columbia, Missouri.

Currently she performs as pianist with the Camerata del Sol Trio, an ensemble she initiated in 2000. Her recordings on Protone and Boston Records are in collaboration with flutist David Aguilar and oboist Evelyn McCarty. She is married to Edgar L. Cortés, pediatrician, who performs in duet recitals with her for benefit events in Corpus Christi where they reside.